Praise for *Stable Recovery*

"This area of horses aiding in substance use disorder recovery is in dire need of a story—especially pertaining to Stable Recovery, Taylor Made Farm, and the Thoroughbred horse industry in Lexington, Kentucky. I believe this is a significant contribution to the field of substance use disorder recovery, reporting on a recovery support service (the power that horses can have on someone recovering from an addiction). I would strongly recommend this book; I think it is very well-written and enjoyable." —**Robin Thompson**, DrPH, MPH, director of Research and Evaluation, Fletcher Group, Inc.

"This book is an engaging and hopeful exploration of lives transformed by the horse—the creature who helped build this country now helps to rebuild souls. These men in recovery, who have not been shown compassion and care, are perhaps the best individuals to bestow that consideration on horses who offer them purpose and acceptance in return. I found the description of Stable Recovery significant and affecting. This would be a valuable addition to libraries across the country, and it does not have geographic limitations." —**JuliAnna Ávila**, associate professor of English, University of North Carolina at Charlotte

"Ken Snyder has poured his heart and soul into *Stable Recovery: How Horses Transform Homeless Men Into Horsemen*. This book is a clear testament to his deep belief in the healing power of horses and the important role that horses have played in the lives of those recovering from addiction and other adversities. Thank you, Ken, for sharing the stories of these men and the horses who helped them." —**Leif Hallberg**, author of *Walking the Way of the Horse: Exploring the Power of the Horse-Human Relationship*

"'You have to submit completely.' That is the first lesson at Stable Recovery. In the book of the same name, the author parallels the unmanageable power of a majestic Thoroughbred racehorse with the struggle of addiction, revealing a transformative path. It chronicles a journey of deep humility where men forge a unique relationship with their Higher Power, achieving a 94 percent sobriety rate and finding new purpose and connection in the process. I'm excited to hear more about the journey of Stable Recovery and the satellites planned at other Kentucky horse farms for both men and women." —**Jan Pollema**, executive director, Hearts & Horses Therapeutic Riding Center

STABLE RECOVERY

New Directions in the Human-Animal Bond

A dynamic relationship has always existed between people and animals. Each influences the psychological and physiological state of the other. Published in collaboration with Purdue University's College of Veterinary Medicine, New Directions in the Human-Animal Bond expands our knowledge of the interrelationships between people, animals, and their environment. Scholarly works, memoirs, practitioner guides, and books written for a general audience are welcomed on all aspects of human-animal interaction and welfare.

SERIES EDITOR

Alan M. Beck, Purdue University

OTHER TITLES IN THIS SERIES

Second Chances: The Transformative Relationship
Between Incarcerated Youth and Shelter Dogs
Joan K. Dalton

Animal-Assisted Counseling and Psychotherapy: A Clinician's Guide
Linda Chassman Craddock and Ellen Kinney Winston

A History of the Development of Alternatives
to Animals in Research and Testing
John Parascandola

Fine Horses and Fair-Minded Riders: Modern Vaquero Horsemanship
JuliAnna Ávila

My One-Eyed, Three-Legged Therapist: How My Cat Clio Saved Me
Kathy M. Finley

Identity, Gender, and Tracking: The Reality of
Boundaries for Veterinary Students
Jenny R. Vermilya

Dogs and Cats in South Korea: Itinerant Commodities
Julien Dugnoille

STABLE RECOVERY

How Horses Transform
Homeless Men Into Horsemen

Ken Snyder

Purdue University Press / *West Lafayette, Indiana*

Cataloging-in-Publication Data is available from the Library of Congress.

978-1-62671-225-6 (paperback)

978-1-62671-226-3 (epub)

978-1-62671-227-0 (epdf)

Cover credit: Stable Recovery resident and horse having a moment, photograph courtesy of Stable Recovery.

All photographs courtesy of Stable Recovery and Ken Snyder.

Dedicated to and in memory of Josh Bryan

Dedicated also to
Giles Anderson and Nick Godfrey
for opening the paddock gates

Contents

Foreword

My dad, Joe Taylor, was always helping anyone he could. He had compassion for people who were struggling and had a heart for young men, teaching them how to work and work hard. He may have had only a sixth-grade education but he had a veritable PhD in people skills. He lived and loved to help people.

I know he and my mother would be walking three feet off the ground had they lived to see Stable Recovery. As you will read, it is the brainchild of my brother Frank and a recovering addict, ironically named Christian Countzler.

The American dream is almost always measured in the realm of earthly wealth. God blessed my brothers and me with a horse farm, Taylor Made, which is the world's largest consignor of also the world's most expensive horses: Thoroughbreds. The farm's star stallion, Not This Time, earns $250,000 for his owners for every baby he fathers.

The dream of my brother Frank to help those suffering from addiction through our horses rests in another realm . . . a spiritual one.

I met Ken Snyder at a picnic commemorating the first anniversary of Stable Recovery at the farm and we instantly hit it off. It was not his first visit, however. On more than a few mornings he would get up at four in the morning to drive to the farm in Nicholasville from his home in Louisville for "Morning Meditation." At that meeting the "clients"—those seeking recovery from addiction—hear a brief devotional. After that, each does a "check-in"—how they are doing, what are their struggles. Most express gratitude for the program. It might be the most important part of their day.

What happens after the meeting *is* the most important: heading out to work with the horses.

Through some innate, God-given ability, the horses mirror what's going on with humans. They can detect depression, anxiety, and fear almost instantly, well before any therapist could. Working with and just being around horses builds accountability and self-esteem in Stable Recovery clients and gives them a sense of purpose. Most important, as the horses grow to accept the clients, a relationship grows. How and why this works in the hearts and minds of the clients to successfully combat addiction is mysterious and incomprehensible. All anyone knows is that it works.

This book takes you through the pain of people beaten, bruised, and bloodied by background, failed relationships, personal tragedy, and falling into addiction. Ken has sat among the men, sharing his own check-in, unconsciously inviting each person in Stable Recovery into his heart. He feels the pain in the lives of Stable Recovery clients because he has experienced it. It comes through every page of this book, especially the profiles he included.

Ken's book will touch your heart, but it is not melodramatic. Stable Recovery began as a novel experiment and is now proven. Ken writes about the history of the program—the family tragedy that led to Stable Recovery; the God-ordained collaboration between Frank and Christian; and the emotional and also physiological factors involved in recovery.

Ken is a twenty-year veteran of "turf writing," pounding the paths of Thoroughbreds and people in horseracing on various racetracks and satisfying a passion for a sport and its athletes in a number of horse publications. He has also authored two other books. A story he wrote for a British horse racing magazine gave him the idea for this book.

I've been blessed to simply be an observer of this program and see its incorporation into not only Taylor Made Farm but the lives of my family. It has been incredibly rewarding.

Whether you are a horse racing fan, psychologist, or simply a horse lover, Ken's book will be rewarding to you, as well.

—**DUNCAN TAYLOR**, *FOUNDER, TAYLOR MADE FARM/*
SENIOR THOROUGHBRED CONSULTANT

Preface

This book began as a magazine and web story entitled "Stable Recovery: How Horses Are Helping Drug Addicts and Alcoholics Build New Lives" (*Gallop* magazine, #43 Q2 2023; *Thoroughbred Racing Commentary* website, June 12th, 2023). I'll never know this for certain, of course, but there might be a similarity to pregnancy between the story and then a book idea—a lot of excitement at what lay ahead and watching it take shape and then the pain of combing a finished text over and over before completion.

Far beyond a magazine article on the subject is a hope that this book will generate incremental income for the Stable Recovery (SR) program beyond current contributions and fundraising. If it generates one penny for the program, then that is one penny that went for something amazingly successful and potentially beneficial for countless people.

The story's subhead introduction, written presumably by my editor at *Gallop* and *TRC*, Nicholas Godfrey, best explains exactly what this book is about: "A ground-breaking program linked to Taylor Made Farm, the world's largest Thoroughbred consignor, is repairing broken lives by helping addicts to find sobriety—and training them for a new future working within the horse industry."

In looking up the dates of publication of the story in *Gallop* and *TRC*, I was surprised that it appeared on the website as recently as June 2023—surprised because, at the time of writing, September 2024, the first draft of the book is complete. The gestation for this baby seems far less than normal.

The reason it's happened quickly, I believe, is that this is a book that needs writing and the sooner the better. My start with this book was a struggle, not in the writing but in budgeting the time. I was busy with articles for the publications just mentioned along with two other magazines, *North American Trainer,* to which I'm a regular contributor, and an annual Kentucky Derby assignment for *Kentucky Monthly* magazine.

A sudden decision to move from a horseless area of western Kentucky (horseless to Thoroughbreds, anyway, excepting Ellis Park in Henderson) to Louisville and closer proximity to horses cost me time that ate into a generous deadline. I had to get on my proverbial horse to get 'er done, as they say in these parts, taking a hiatus from magazine writing to get cracking and finish what you now hold in your hands.

Both content and inspiration came from trips to see family in Louisville from Kuttawa in western Kentucky. While in Louisville, there would be more than a few mornings I'd get up at 4:00 a.m. for a one-hour-and-fifteen-minute drive to Nicholasville, Kentucky, just south of Lexington, to Taylor Made Farm for Morning Meditation with the men of SR. That was a daily 6:00 a.m. meeting that A.A.ers would recognize as a check-in meeting.

It was a priority to make the meeting to see and meet these men. To be in their company and see lives touched by Stable Recovery also touched me deeply. I only wish I lived closer so I could be at more of the meetings.

I would suggest something a bit odd but valuable and deeply moving: go to one or more A.A. meetings, ideally two different ones. (Some are better than others.) The experience will explain why. All you religious folks gather your rocks right now for throwing because I will say straight-up that most A.A. meetings are what church is supposed to be.

Church is for the sick, not for those pretending to be well. Morning Meditation, based on the Twelve Steps of Alcoholics Anonymous, is a fantastic church. Men find there what they need daily. Community. Support. Sharing. Vulnerability. Trust. Connection.

That last one is key: the opposite of addiction is connection. This book is about the connection of horses to men who need it most.

Acknowledgments

I have to go back more than a few years to thank my editor/publisher at *Trainer* magazine, Giles Anderson. He showed great understanding and grace during a rough patch in my life some years ago when I needed a hiatus from writing. I pray and believe I came back from the hiatus not just a better man, but a better writer. Many thanks, Giles.

Thanks, too, to Christopher Smith, retired editor of the British magazine *Gallop*. Anyone who picks up a copy of this magazine would see it is completely dazzling even if you have no interest in horses or horse racing. I have neighbors who devour copies who have never been to a racetrack or even a horse farm. For a turf writer to be a contributor to *Gallop* is a privilege and an honor, especially for someone from the southern West Virginia coalfields. Chris launched my relationship with the magazine with a first story comparing the cost of jockey equipment and horse tack to that of a professional football player. The hook, surprisingly, was the higher cost to outfit and equip a jockey.

Chris's successor as editor, Nicholas Godfrey, has enabled me to continue with *Gallop* and venture into writing pieces for a column. He has done this while tolerating queries submitted at the wrong times, which I know bugs him, but he tolerates me . . . so far. He is a highly gifted writer and an author whose use of one word, "thoughtfully," in a sentence about graffiti on a sign pointing to the barbershop at Aqueduct racetrack in New York, is the single funniest thing I've ever read. He and Giles gave me entrée into horse racing. Without that, I could not have authored this book.

Many thanks also to my editor at Purdue University Press, Andrea Kathryn Gapsch. Heretofore, I thought all nonfiction books involved writing the first three chapters and a proposal. Publishing with a university press disabused me of that belief quickly; that's for nonfiction with non-university publishers. It's the whole enchilada, and *then* you find out if you've wasted months and months, more months, and even years, just like it is with novelists. Andrea was kind enough to indulge an "innocent" read of the first three chapters, then give me a nonbinding, informal go-ahead. (I blew off another possible book with another university publisher when it was all or nothing.)

I want to also thank Dr. Ann Baldwin, professor emerita of physiology at the University of Arizona. She is a Brit, along with Giles, Nick, and Chris mentioned above, who was a key contributor in explaining a phenomenon in horse-human relationships that is astonishing and not easily grasped. Many, many thanks, Dr. Baldwin, for taking a complex subject and explaining it beautifully. The Afterword of this book was not possible without you. God save the King!

Lastly, I owe everything to all of the people connected with Taylor Made Farm and Stable Recovery (SR). The profiles of individuals in this book transformed by the program required courage and vulnerability rare in a world of mostly insecure, fainthearted people. To all of the men profiled, to all of the staff at Taylor Made and SR, and to the board of SR, my sincere and deepest thanks.

I am most indebted to Frank Taylor and Christian Countzler, cofounders of SR. They are two extraordinary and truly great men guided, I believe, by hearts and minds anointed by God. It was and is a blessing to just meet and know Christian and Frank, much less write a book about them.

Frank comes from "good stock," as they say, which applies, of course, to brothers Duncan, Mark, and Ben. Taylor Made Farm is a leader in the Thoroughbred industry through a family taught extremely well by a Bluegrass legend, their father, Joe Taylor. SR is part of a legacy from a man, father, and horseman who was hugely admired and highly respected.

Unforgettable, for me, was Frank getting wind that I was on the farm doing a story for *Gallop* and asking that I come by the farm's office to talk with him. When you spend your time chasing down interviewees, the majority of whom never return calls and texts, Frank's invite was shocking and deeply appreciated. I know, after being around him, that that's Frank—marvelously spontaneous and immeasurably kind. I have to think the time he gave me that day had everything to do with a magazine story evolving into a book.

He once introduced me to some friends, telling them I came to the farm for a story and left ten days later. I appreciated him saying that, and what he communicated is something I'll always treasure. He has made me feel more than an observer of SR but a part of it. That's Frank being Frank.

The truth is, I left a part of my heart there. Yes, I describe myself as a "word schlep," but I also know God directed my steps to Frank, Christian, and men in the program who are living, breathing miracles.

The only way I can thank Christian Countzler is to say about him that he is who I would want my son to become. There's nobody I admire more as a man. What he has overcome in life is beyond remarkable. It is amazing and God-given. But even though it is, Christian had to make a choice to accept the recovery path offered to him. Because he did accept it, hundreds of men needing to tread that same path will do so. It is important for me to express this here because he is too busy unconsciously and beautifully *giving away what he cannot keep to gain what he cannot lose.*

Finally, I need to thank my wife, Cassie. I read every chapter I complete aloud because that's a foolproof way of catching things easily missed when reading silently. It also helps me to accept reluctantly and with ambiguity her label for me as "geeky nerd" as a compliment. I love you, Bootsie.

Introduction

And I saw, and behold a white horse . . . and a crown
was given unto him . . .

REV. 6:2

Some horse people with a religious bent see Divine significance in the white horse in the Book of Revelation. That's for you to decide. Without knowing or researching it, I suspect the Quran, the Bhagavad Gita, and so forth include horses, too. The question is why the Messiah in Christianity would ride a horse. The bigger issue is the obvious inference (revelation?) that there are evidently horses in heaven.

There wasn't any intention with this book to point to the Divine in the stories of the horses and the men who care for them. What happens between horse and human is mysterious. The relationships demand looking into the spiritual for understanding. Leif Hallberg's excellent book *Walking the Way of the Horse* (2008) addresses the spiritual component in an analytical, comprehensive, and extensively researched examination of horse-human relationships. It is fair to say that modern psychology, at least in regard to horses, includes the spiritual in looking at these relationships. It has to, and Chapter 10 of the book you are currently reading includes it.

Why does the Stable Recovery (SR) program achieve a ninety-day sobriety rate as high as 94 percent compared to the national percentage for live-in rehabilitation facilities' pitifully low 12 percent? The answer is as elusive as trying to bottle fog in a jar: something happens between horse and human. But what is it? One answer—and it is a big one—lies in the stories of formerly homeless drug addicts and alcoholics profiled individually in Part 2 of this book.

Part 1 presents the origins of SR: the family crisis that brought it about; the horrific past life of one of the two founders; and the collaboration of two men gifted with rare compassion, instinct, drive, generosity, and intelligence.

What has come from SR in its brief history (eighteen months at the time of writing) has the potential to produce a sea change in how professionals approach and help homeless addicts. Horses have long been instrumental in therapy for autistic children and the incarcerated. This book introduces the application of horses in therapy for the first time to persons who may need it most: the homeless. It uncovers astonishing and incredibly touching behavior by Thoroughbreds and equally amazing results.

I sincerely hope I am qualified to take on the task of authoring a book about this program. I am a turf writer, which has zero to do with agronomy. It is the label given to writers covering the sport of horse racing. I don't write about race results or the daily events like the majority of turf writers. Instead, I cover issues beyond the day-to-day and behind the scenes. Stories, for example, have been on the high percentage of Black trainers and exercise riders who are Louisiana natives, most from Cajun Country; business issues such as Canadian incentives to native trainers to breed in that country; and participatory journalism that included (for about a half hour) my career as a licensed hot walker. (Horses need walking to cool down after a workout or race so muscles don't contract or "tie up" and for heartbeat and respiration to come back to resting levels.)

A magazine story birthed this book, as noted in the Preface. The importance of the program, though, warrants more than a publication thrown away in a month or two. I've written this book for general readers, but it is my hope that it can be useful to academicians and addiction rehabilitation professionals. It could prove to be.

My own personal horse-human relationship began with fandom as you will read about in Chapter 9. That evolved into a full-blown love-at-first-sight moment when a baby Thoroughbred, somewhere between a year and two years old, walked away from his groom and up to me out of curiosity. It was my first contact with a Thoroughbred. The moment was both life-changing and career-changing.

It led to my aforementioned hotwalking. Before that, I was an owner of four horses (not together). That's not as grandiose as it may sound; my ownership was micro-shares that gave me as much of a thrill as a millionaire mogul gets from sole ownership and investment in a Thoroughbred costing hundreds of thousands of dollars.

With my first horse, I calculated I owned about six pounds of Moon Unit, who finished an eighteen-race career on the Maryland/West Virginia racing circuit.

His beginnings on racetracks like the Fair Grounds in New Orleans and Keeneland in Lexington came through an outstanding pedigree. His grandsire (grandfather, for the uninitiated) A.P. Indy won both the Belmont Stakes and Breeders' Cup Classic. He was Horse of the Year in 1992. His racetrack earnings? A cool $2.9 million. His dam (mother), Holiday Soirée, was the daughter of a stallion who won $3.6 million on the racetrack.

The formula for Thoroughbred breeding is repeated often: Breed the best to the best and hope for the best. More times than not, though, the best isn't forthcoming no matter the ability of sire or dam.

Somewhere in a string of fifteen losses in a row for Moon Unit, I came on board as a micro-owner. A couple of races later a trainer at Charles Town Races in West Virginia claimed him, or bought him out of a race, despite a winless record. That ended my ownership and that of other shareholders. He got his first win soon after that, naturally. Typical luck for me.

In his first start for the stable, of which I was a part, I was as excited as if he were running in the Kentucky Derby. I couldn't believe it myself, but starting on Wednesday, any thought of the race on Saturday tied my stomach in knots. I had no idea I would get so wound up with anticipation, and it was a complete delight. I look back with great fondness on telling my wife in the middle of our Saturday religious service that I had to go to the bathroom. Go to the bathroom my ass. I had to go check my phone to see how my horse ran.

He lost, of course, but I learned having even a small, small piece of a Thoroughbred racehorse was as much fun as you can have with your clothes on. (More on that below.) It was the best $149 I ever spent, and the $9.90 Moon Unit somehow earned for me is a treasure. I still have the check in my backpack. It will go uncashed.

I've had more than one person tell me that seeing your horse coming down the stretch to win a race really is better than sex. Moon Unit came close to winning his first race right after I bought my micro-share, and I've never been more excited for a sports event. And were it not for the jockey inexplicably guiding him to the rail where the track was deepest and slowest, and complete blindness on the part of the track stewards to an obvious foul by another horse, he might have won. (A trainer friend on the racetrack told me ownership, small though it may be, had made me an instant asshole.) I have no idea how I would have responded had he finished first. I'm sure it would have involved a bottle of champagne and sex—the latter to verify the claim of other horse owners, of course.

I had thought running races and earning money were the most important things Thoroughbreds did, followed by breeding offspring that also ran and earned money.

Running and running fast, however, cannot compare to a capability within them away from the racetrack. It manifests in the barns and paddocks of Taylor Made Farm in the heart of Kentucky's Bluegrass Region with formerly homeless drug and alcohol addicts.

This book, in Part 1, chronicles this: how the SR program evolved, the scope, the therapists, and, most important, the effectiveness. Part 2 is the story of twelve men who owe their sobriety and recovery, if not their lives, to Thoroughbreds.

Their stories are minimally edited. All are tragic, detailing, in some instances, horrendous experiences and unimaginable hardship. The experiences speak for themselves. Talking through those experiences took courage for the men. They were also disclosed unconsciously to help others. My task was stitching together the pieces, something that moved me, many times, to tears when I would finish a chapter.

Only another homeless person can know what it is to endure a winter living in a tent on the banks of the Ohio River, or to walk down roads and streets kicking bottles and cans to see if there is anything in them to drink. Only another homeless person can understand why desperation for these men was considered a gift.

On occasion, the men cried while telling their stories—some in gratitude for survival, others remembering the things that made them addicted and homeless, and some whose recovery broke through virtual catatonia to long-buried emotions.

Their stories are sacred, as is their recovery. They are testimonies to the goodness of God; the inner strength of men who have embraced a tough, ultra-demanding program; and the wondrous, mysterious power of horses.

I've both lived and written long enough to know we all have a story, and all are worthy of telling and hearing. But there are some stories that, if you are pumping blood, will touch you deeply. The word "miracle" might be a cliché to describe many of the things that happened in the lives of the men of SR. I'll let you be the judge. Each story has a happy ending, but not happy enough to just leave behind quickly. Their stories plumb the unfathomable and unforgettable. There are happy endings but they are shadowed by what went before. That is as it should be. The good and the bad are the whole truth.

The horses might be the only completely positive part of this book. They give what is not asked for. They don't know, of course, someone's prison record or addiction. But they will sense a need and respond to it.

I'll tease you with the story of one horse and a harrowing experience for a former trainer and close friend of mine. Frank took his four-year-old son to the racetrack and got the scare of his life. In the barn area, my friend's son got away from him unnoticed and toddled into the stall of a horse that fit every negative stereotype for a

Thoroughbred—difficult, uncooperative, hostile to handlers, a biter, *and* a kicker—a horse that was legitimately dangerous. So bad was this horse, he had even earned an orange cone parked a few feet from his stall door, warning passersby to not get close to him. Very few horses are bad enough to require an orange cone boundary.

Frank looked into the stall to see his son standing underneath this horse. That horse, the meanest on that racetrack, knew not to hurt the toddler.

In SR, horses do more than not harm humans. They heal.

Part 1

The Story of Stable Recovery

Well hell, let's do it.
—FRANK TAYLOR

1

The Legacy of Joe Taylor

*Make time for doing charity or volunteer work
or whatever is in your power to make this a
better world.*
—JOSEPH LANNON TAYLOR, *JOE TAYLOR'S COMPLETE
GUIDE TO BREEDING AND RAISING RACEHORSES*

Horses can hear a human's heartbeat from four feet away.

They can also know what is *in* a human's heart.

They have proven it with the last people in the world you would expect: homeless men suffering from substance addiction and alcoholism. The most remarkable thing is where they do it—at one of the world's most noted Thoroughbred farms not only in Kentucky but in the world, with horses that are some of the most expensive on the planet.

How a human's heart-function factors in with the effect horses have on homeless men emotionally, spiritually, and psychologically is unknown. Physiological changes in humans, however, are real. (More about this in Chapter 10.) There is still much we may never know—specifically, why and how these changes take place. What we *do* know is that Thoroughbreds and homeless men working together pierce the power of drug and alcohol addiction at a rate that is astonishing and never seen before.

That Taylor Made Farm would birth and be home to Stable Recovery (SR) is a combination of circumstances, hard work, and also a willingness to see if something works.

Innovation is not new to Taylor Made and the Taylor brothers. The farm may have been the first in Kentucky to introduce what the oldest Taylor brother, Duncan, called a customer-centric approach to client relations and the first to embrace marketing practices now copied by probably ever other farm in the industry. Taylor Made was the first consignor to send videos and photos of horses to customers. Marketing, however, was in another universe from entrusting horses worth hundreds of thousands of dollars to homeless men. It was a long shot but one that "came in," as they say of winners at the racetrack.

The horses do more than know what is in a human's heart. The physiological and emotional changes in the hearts of men are rooted in something unique but until now largely overlooked in addiction rehabilitation: meaningful work far removed from asking "Do you want fries with that order?" or mind-numbing factory labor. Important, challenging, and, to an extent, risky work transforms the men of SR. The work brings together hurting men who have difficulty with humans finding connection and relationship. With the horses and the men it is as if the ability is built in.

Many of the horses know to extend grace and kindness to those who have never received it. They will sense fear in a human and, contrary to the stereotype (particularly with Thoroughbreds) that they will bully someone fearful, they will often give humans a pass on kicks and bites and respond with understanding of that fear, with kindness and cooperation. They have amazing intuition that enables them to somehow pick up on everything from a temporary mood to a character defect of a human. They are a barometer for a human's state of mind, reflecting exactly the behavior and attitude of a human to help that person see it and correct it.

The bottom line is they can give to a person, a drug addict or alcoholic, something that another human cannot give. It's inexplicable. It's spiritual. It's mystical. It is real.

MUCH OF THE STORY OF SR IS ABOUT THE COLLABORATION OF FRANK TAYLOR, joint owner with three brothers of Taylor Made Farm, and of Christian Countzler, president and CEO. Frank, who, at the time of writing, had recently retired from a role as general manager of the farm, freely admits to alcoholism in former days. Christian was an alcoholic and drug addict who was homeless for three years.

To understand Frank Taylor and his brothers—Duncan, Mark, and Ben—and really, the genesis of Taylor Made Farm and the seed for SR, you have to go back to their father, Joe Taylor. Joe was a classic Kentucky "hardboot" and a legendary horseman who authored a definitive book on Thoroughbred care quoted in the opening to this chapter.

The term "hardboot," according to Kentucky lore, comes from dew-hardened boots worn by men out in the fields of central Kentucky—working-class men who built the columned antebellum mansions that dot this incredibly picturesque landscape. Others, Irish immigrants skilled in piecing stones together to make fences in their homeland, came to do the same in Kentucky. Those fences still stand just as they were on the day the stones were laid more than a century and a half ago.

The Taylors, obviously, aren't the blueblood aristocracy that makes up the majority of horse farm owners in the Bluegrass. Joe was Roman Catholic but expressed his religion not in words, but in deeds. The formal stuff—dinner table catechism—was the task of the boys' mom.

Joe's faith, however, manifested in something all four sons will tell you in one way or another: "Dad was always helping somebody," said Duncan Taylor. If "faith without works is dead," according to the Book of James 2:14 in the New Testament, Joe Taylor checked that box again and again and again.

He made his bones at Gainesway Farm in Lexington as farm manager for dog food magnate John Gaines. He built Taylor Made Farm after hours at Gainesway, often using the headlights of pickup trucks parked strategically at dusk to light whatever could be done before leaving for the night. And if his sons were old enough to pitch in, they were side by side with their dad.

Farm managers like Joe Taylor do not make the headlines or news in Thoroughbred racing. That's left up to the farm owners and the trainers they select for their horses and the jockeys who ride them.

On Thoroughbred racing's biggest day—Kentucky Derby Day— owners will be in box seats at Churchill Downs and trainers of Derby entrants will put on expensive suits they will wear, in some cases, only for Derby Day. For farm managers, it is another workday. They are back on the farm making sure horses get their feed and care just like all the other 364 days of the year—Christmas and Thanksgiving.

Joe Taylor was born with compassion for others that he, himself, needed to receive. The family experienced two tragedies that moved and motivated Joe to show his four sons a path that became Taylor Made Farm.

"I had an older brother, Dan Marshall Taylor, who was killed in a car wreck. He was eighteen," said Duncan Taylor, a second son born after Dan.

Another son after Duncan also died. This death was harder on Joe Taylor and his wife than that of the oldest son because of the manner of death. He was a murder victim.

"My brother Chris was running a farm and had hired some labor to help us. One of the guys who moved in was part of a bunch of riffraff— people who'd never had any training," said Duncan.

"Chris came home one night and saw a gate off its hinges. Stuff had been stolen before, so he went back there and one of the guys was drunk and shot him.

"One guy was near passed out, laying with the gun across his body. He was probably totally out of it and didn't know what he was doing."

Joe and his wife worked through their grief with their own methods and at their own pace. "My mom was like a rock," Duncan said.

"'Oh Joe, it was God's will,' she would say," Duncan recalled. "'You have to understand that and accept it and go on. You've got other kids you gotta raise. You can't be dwelling on this.'" Duncan overheard this more than a few times.

"My dad would go out there [the farm where Chris's murder took place] and I'd go with him. He'd drive around to look where he'd gotten killed and he'd ask the same questions: 'What do you think happened? Why this?'" Duncan said.

Joe Taylor drew from the deaths of his two sons a simple lesson but one that goes unlearned for most families: stick together closely. He knew family and family togetherness should come first, that they mean far more than money or who gets the credit for success. Specifically, he urged his sons to unite and work and build something . . . that they could achieve greater success together rather than separately.

"He'd tell stories about these brothers who had a welding company and an iron company, and how they stuck together. Nobody could compete with them. He was pointing out that staying together was good.

"He was telling us that before we even had a business," Duncan recounted.

The lesson Joe took probably came, deep down, from the loss of two sons. There is no guarantee of another day. Car wrecks happen. Murders happen less often, but they do occur. You may have a brother one day who is gone the next. Keep them close. He drilled into his sons to go into business together. As it turned out, he was right.

Duncan believes his dad bought land in Jessamine County to build Taylor Made Farm as a legacy for his sons. At the same time, it was a means for Joe to get his mind off the deaths of his sons and work through his grief. A land purchase of 190 acres for $600 an acre and paying off the $114,000 debt can also tend to crowd out other issues. It's what gets successful entrepreneurs up in the morning probably after fitful sleep.

Duncan, who was driving a tractor and bush-hogging fields at age twelve, learned his own lesson from the development of the land near Nicholasville, Kentucky, just south of Lexington.

"Somebody who's really interested in something—somebody who's looking at it every day and trying to be really involved and stay right on top of something—that probably has as much to do with success as anything."

The Taylor boys were supporting their family with Taylor Made Farm. It *had* to be a success.

Duncan offers a modest reason Taylor Made has become what it is in the horse industry: "We probably have one of the best organized horse farms that there is, but that's just because I think a lot of people who own horse farms, they do it as a hobby, and it's not their primary business. They don't put as much thought into it."

Taylor Made is, as the name states, *Taylor made*. Sweat equity built it, and after God and family, the farm was and is everything to the brothers. Its history includes striving to recruit and develop workers. A precursor to SR was a program called Caring Team that aimed simply at making the farm and the workplace better for its employees.

What would Joe Taylor say about SR? Without hesitation, Duncan responds, "It makes business sense, and it also makes sense for your faith."

Responsibilities and roles float between the four brothers. Frank engineered something that was faith in action *and* made business sense. His three brothers signed off on SR.

The risk involved in hiring homeless addicts was not as great as it may seem. "You go out in the general population; you're probably hiring addicts anyway. They're just not in recovery," said Duncan Taylor with a shrug.

The advent of SR was classic Frank Taylor, according to Duncan. "He shoots from the hip. 'I'm going to get this done.' The rest are details."

With affection, Duncan made this observation about his younger brother: "He's not a planner. Any planning going on in SR is because somebody else is forcing him to do it."

Duncan also knows that Frank possesses an entrepreneurial spirit that seems to come naturally to him. "He's practical in wanting to make a profit, and he knows the people able to bring it about."

Frank Taylor is the co-founder and point of the spear of SR. Ironically, the idea for it was his response to a family tragedy of his own that you'll read about in Chapter 3. Like father, like son. As his father built a farm, Frank would build upon it an incredible program.

Maybe he was taking an unconscious cue from his dad or maybe it is in his DNA, but Frank responded to his own family tragedy with an idea he had that would help both the farm and others. Anyone who knew Joe Taylor wouldn't be surprised probably.

Christian Countzler was the perfect person for SR, and his experience, talents, and drive were instantly apparent to Frank. He and Frank are co-founders of SR. At the time of writing, Christian is also SR's first president and CEO.

Like any business, there are distinct functions. Operations produce what the business has to sell. Management supervises production and subsequent sales and marketing.

In the context of SR, horses are the operations division, producing recovery. Men like Frank and Christian are management, overseeing transfer of recovery from horse to man and maximizing it in both numbers and effectiveness. Success in this endeavor or business hinges on the success and lasting value of the product.

Why and how the horses produce recovery is the answer to a question known only to a Higher Power, to borrow recovery jargon from the Twelve Steps of Alcoholics Anonymous. They are the unlikeliest of heroes.

In a world of homelessness, suicide, deaths from overdoses, and other tragedies, what Frank and Christian have created is a bright spot that penetrates the darkness. It began, though, with Joe Taylor.

2

Horses and the "It Factor"

*There is something about the outside of a horse that
is good for the inside of a man.*

—WINSTON CHURCHILL

What is that something?

Will Walden, a Thoroughbred trainer based at Keeneland Race Course outside Lexington, Kentucky, summed up in simplest terms a key dynamic between horses and the men that work for him. It provides a glimmer of the *something* inimitable to horses: "It may take a month, it may take two months, it may take four months, but there will come a day when that horse looks them in the eye, and they know they are accepted." He has watched this happen since his stable began in April of 2022.

Acceptance is something most of these men, along with others in Stable Recovery (SR), have never experienced. The majority come from homes where nurturing and acceptance, usually from a father, were missing.

SR houses men and trains them in horsemanship for jobs like those in Will Walden's Ready Made Racing stable. Other jobs and potential careers follow on horse farms, in veterinary equine clinics in Lexington (which bills itself as the Horse Capital of the World), and on the race-track with other trainers besides Will.

The dynamic he speaks of stems from a horse's necessary dependence on a human for feeding, health, and fitness. The men of SR enter a business like Ready Made at the bottom of a hierarchy. Hot walkers, as the name suggests, walk horses after a workout or race to cool them down gradually to prevent muscle contractions after the exertion of running. Horses are walked, too, until pulse and respiration are back to normal. Hot walkers are the lowest step on the ladder. Grooms are the next step up, but a big one. Grooms bathe the horses, brush them to clear dust and dirt from their coats and stimulate blood flow, wrap lower legs, and much more. The best and most successful grooms and hot walkers connect with the horses they care for because they at least like, if not love, them. They had better because they spend more time with the horses than anyone—more than the trainer, assistant trainer, or barn foreman.

Horses are preyed-upon animals with safety always the first thought, especially with anything new. Mares in current times in secure, well-lit barns instinctively foal or birth babies at night. This harkens back to life many, many centuries ago in the wild when wolves and other predators were more likely to attack a foal in daylight.

On the racetrack, loading racehorses onto trailers is the most common aggravation and toughest task, evoking anger and sometimes ill-treatment of animals from handlers. Common sense on the part of humans, typically, is missing. No one ever wonders or asks why a horse balks at loading. It's simply assumed that they're stupid or crazy. It's a Thoroughbred being a Thoroughbred.

If loading a trailer is an adventure for the human assigned the task, it is much more for the horse. They don't know if they are stepping into a bottomless abyss.

It isn't that they are skittish as much as wary to the point of distrust. Safety first.[1]

A horse trusts when they know they are safe. When they know *you*, the human, are safe, the stage is set for healing, sobriety, and a new life.

SR connects horses and men who have desperately needed a connection with something or someone. Horses provide possibly the first healthy relationship that many of these men have ever had. The results are remarkable and even incredible: As many as 94 percent of SR residents have achieved sobriety over ninety days, a statistic that dwarfs the national average of 12 percent for other live-in rehabilitation programs. Sustained recovery is also statistically superior because of what can follow for SR graduates, as you will read.

A relationship between a horse and a human is not automatic or something that is a given. Horses will give you what you didn't ask for, but the human must first be willing to receive it. This is true whether it is a recreational horse to ride or, in a completely different realm, training a Thoroughbred to race or caring for them on a farm.

---

1.   The universal means, unfortunately, of getting a balky horse to load on a trailer is to whip them. An article entitled "Horses With Attitude—The Concept of Behavioral Conditioning in Racehorses" in the January 22nd, 2022, issue of *Trainer* magazine put forth that horses experience the same neurochemical releases of dopamine from punishment as for good behavior. Whipping a horse will reinforce exactly what a handler does not want, continued balking at loading, according to Frank Barnett, a practitioner of what is called "evidence-based horsemanship." Loading horses into a trailer is often difficult for Thoroughbred handlers, particularly with young horses. In their brain, the horse is wondering, *"Am I safe?"* Practically every horse, at least the first time, will balk. It's a strange, unfamiliar environment. In the horse's mind, they might think they're getting a big shove off a cliff or into a black hole.

The remedy is minor stress followed by quiet, according to Barnett. "You bring the horse up to the trailer and give him a nudge. He backs out of there. 'Nope. I'm not going.' So, he turns away and you [the handler] go with him. But as soon as he turns around to leave the trailer, I get him bothered. I'll walk him in circles. I'll cause him some confusion and discomfort. His mind is racing, and he can't figure out where comfort is.

"I'm not talking about twitching his ear or inflicting pain but making it so he can't find relief or peace any place since leaving the trailer.

"Then I guide him back to the trailer. The closer he gets to it, the quieter I get. It's like he's escaping from all the chaos by going to the trailer. He'll get on."

Kyle Berryman, who serves as assistant trainer to Will Walden, had wariness and distrust a lot like a horse when he was using drugs. He had watched humanity walk by and ignore him as he sat on city sidewalks. Most of the time, his only interaction with a sober human was a tray of food passed wordlessly by a volunteer at a shelter kitchen. Therapists were the only source of anything resembling conversation with someone from the outside world, repeating rote questions and timeworn bromides. Sustained sobriety has been a whole new experience for Kyle, achieved through an unlikely source.

"The bond I share with the horses is like no other," he said. "If you really don't feel like dealing with humans that day, you go in and start grooming a horse. I know they're listening. I can feel it. I can see it in their eyes.

"These horses, they rely on us. I take pride in that. When you take one up to the paddock for a race, there are those minutes where I'm thinking of nothing but what is going on right then and there. That's not how my past has been. It's been ten miles in the future or ten miles in the past. But now I can finally feel being in the moment, and that's precious to me."

That moment puts Kyle in a position of responsibility, the weight of which is both literal and figurative. He oversees a half-ton animal that can easily overpower him if it so desires. The task for the handler is to be in control and command of an obvious mismatch. It demands a commitment to that moment, setting aside the regret of the past or thoughts of a dismal future. It is an undertaking without room for daydreaming or inattention of any kind. But it is also an opportunity to embrace purpose, achievement, and a huge measure of self-esteem.

I heard a young teacher say, "The starting place for contentment is commitment to purpose. Why is that important? Because the alternative is comparison to people. If someone is always comparing himself or herself to others, it is inevitable they will feel less than." With the homeless, comparing themselves to others is shattering.

Feeling *less than* makes the world and the people in it unsafe for someone with a substance abuse disorder. You become a nonparticipant in a world that is out of control for you, that has proven too much to handle. Horses in the wild, on the other hand, adapt and learn coping lessons in a sometimes dangerous environment where they are the hunted.

Horses will repeatedly interrupt drinking from a stream or pond to scan the horizon for a predator animal. Addicts merely survive, if you can call it that, temporarily escaping reality and a real life with drugs and alcohol. Full escape and a kind of surrender to hopelessness is homelessness.

Horses, again, can hear the heartbeat of a human from four feet away. The more amazing thing, however, is intuitiveness with humans and their ability to even express concern for a human handler, as unbelievable as that may sound from a one-thousand-pound animal. "What you think, they feel," said Tyler Maxwell, a former exercise rider for Walden's string of horses who now does the same at WinStar Farm outside Lexington. "If you're walking around with a 'low head,' worried about yourself and how miserable your life is, you're going to pass that on to these horses. If you keep things light and positive and happy, that energy passes on to them."

The shedrow (the path in front of the stalls in a Thoroughbred racing barn) illustrates this. "If you walked down the Ready Made shedrow at any given time, the horses aren't standing in the back of their stalls with their ears pinned back. They are out at the stall door bobbing their heads and looking for attention."

Tyler is a loquacious thirty-two-year-old who compressed what is normally three years of training to learn exercise riding into one year, according to Walden. His enthusiasm and energy seem boundless.

He loves the horses he rides, but he has also come to love those working beside him in the barn because he knows and has experienced their struggles as addicts.

"It's not about me. It's about the new guys coming in. Now when I lay my head down at the end of the day, I know that I've tried and done my best to help these guys.

"Never in a million years did I think I'd be where I am today, entrusted with these horses. It's been a heckuva journey."

Barn life *is* life for Tyler. "I'd do this for free," he said with a laugh.

Tyler had ridden before coming to Kentucky, but almost all of the men of SR have never touched a horse. Some, in the words of Frank Taylor, are "naturals" and others who aren't "can become very good horsemen if they try really hard."

The former has "horse piss in their veins" or a "horse gene," as horsemen and horsewomen say. Others will have to overcome fear, not as much of a challenge as you might think, even with the most high-strung Thoroughbreds or nervous human. More importantly, they will have to *appreciate* a horse—their quirks, their very distinct personalities, their individuality. A former jockey, whose career spanned parts of twenty-nine years and over twenty thousand races, once told me that every horse has their own gait, their own rhythm different from every other runner. No two are alike. The same applies to personalities in horses just as with people.

Unforgettable for me was watching a particularly good racehorse prepare for a gallop in the darkness one morning with his trainer. He told me to "just watch." The horse bounced around a bit under his exercise rider before finally moving into a gallop. "He does this every morning; he hates to train," the trainer said with a smile. The habit was not a source of annoyance for this trainer. That was just the horse being *himself*. The trainer appreciated that horse. There was obvious fondness.

How does this bond that Kyle Berryman talked about or Tyler Maxwell's willingness to work for free happen? Is it that *something* that Churchill talked about?

Frank Taylor can tell you what it is. He, along with the ironically named Christian Countzler, had the idea for SR. Frank knew the "it factor" with horses would help men find purpose, especially hurting, addicted men. The next chapter of this book is Frank's story, which includes family tragedy and life as a functioning alcoholic.

3

Basement Epiphanies and Giving Back

You mean you think *you're an alcoholic?*

—FRANK TAYLOR

Think Kentucky horseman and many people will picture a goateed old man like the late Colonel Sanders of fried chicken fame, a genteel type in a white linen suit.

Frank Taylor couldn't be further from that picture. He's a tad on the stout side, and there's something out of kilter to see him in a suit and tie or tuxedo for a special event. It's just not Frank.

His countenance might make you think of an adult Tom Sawyer. There's a very slight gap between his front teeth that you will see much of because he smiles a lot. A gleam in his eyes completes the picture. The smile is genuine and comes from finding peace in his life through sobriety.

He didn't always have that peace. In past times, the party didn't start until Frank got there, but an exuberant, hail-fellow-well-met personality and demeanor came largely from a bottle. Now, the source is a love of life and the people seeking freedom from addiction. He'll talk to anybody, no matter their station in life. He addresses maintenance staff on his farm by their first names because he's taken the time to get to know them. He's also comfortable talking to sheikhs and oil barons from the Middle East.

Frank Taylor is a farm boy, for sure, and you can't take the farm out of the boy. He works at the eponymously named Taylor Made Farm with his three brothers. It is a farm, but the term somehow seems inadequate. It is a thousand acres of prime central Kentucky land that is home to approximately eight hundred Thoroughbred horses. And they are not just any horses but sleek, extremely beautiful horses bred to run like the wind. They have made Taylor Made a global company, hence the relationships with some of the wealthiest people on the planet.

Taylor Made Farm has grown from a small boarding farm into the worldwide leader in Thoroughbred sales and marketing, to borrow from the farm's website. The farm has sold more Grade 1 winners, Breeders' Cup champions, and million-dollar sale-toppers than competitors and annually ranks atop the world's leading sales agencies. Taylor Made also is a breeding center with some of the top stallions in the world. One example is Not This Time, who earned for his owners $135,000 for every successful breeding in 2023. (Success means the foal stood and nursed after its birth.) In 2026, breeding a mare to Not This Time costs $250,000. That means potential earnings of $50 million.

For many of us traversing this region of central Kentucky, known famously as the Bluegrass, and passing Taylor Made Farm, envy and coveting might be expected. "They're printing their own money," is the thought and assumption. And if you met Frank, you'd also assume his countenance comes from financial security. Nothing could be further from the truth.

Wealth does not mean an absence of woes . . . sometimes big ones.

One aspect of the kind of wealth Frank Taylor has earned is that it means more decisions. Slowly and imperceptibly for many people, it can steal joy and crowd out the most important things in life—family and faith. Frank would tell you he's always had faith, but not like what he has now. He would definitely tell you that he, like probably everyone, has experienced dysfunction in his immediate family.

Frank's life didn't just take a detour in 2020 but hit a Road Closed, a metaphorical mountain highway buried under a mudslide that stopped everything in his life. Returning home from a vacation with his wife, Kim, they couldn't find their then twenty-year-old son, Chris. He wasn't where he should have been—kitchen, bedroom, or den. Frank took the steps downstairs to the basement to a discovery that was life-changing for both him and his son.

Chris had assembled a makeshift barricade. It was an unconscious representation of the isolation of addiction and also a wordless cry for help that elicited from Frank the question Chris needed to hear from his father at that moment: "What's wrong?"

"I'm an alcoholic."

"You mean you *think* you're an alcoholic?"

"No. I *know* I am an alcoholic," his son replied. "I've been drinking a handle of vodka a day for two years." (A handle meaning a half gallon. "Handle" is slang—the bottle's volume requires one.)

Neither Frank nor Kim had ever seen Chris drunk, but with the secret exposed, they started searching the basement and other rooms to find bottles everywhere.

Frank and Kim did what any good parents would do. They sought help for their son, sending him to "maybe four rehabs," according to Frank.

Frank also decided he needed to do something before going back up the stairs from the basement: never take a drink of an alcoholic beverage again.

"I'd been a heavy drinker for years and I always wondered if I was an alcoholic," Frank said, finally facing the fact he was a *functioning* alcoholic but an alcoholic, nonetheless.

"I kept my family together or I kept my job, a real big business. But I wasn't happy or fulfilled.

"I used to have fun drinking the first couple of decades, and then the next two decades it got worse and worse. There was no fun in it. Hangovers started lasting three days instead of three hours. And so, if you drink heavy twice a week, you're hungover most of the time. I was kind of in that state."

A devout Roman Catholic, Frank had sworn off drinking for Lent every year for over what he estimated at thirty years. "It lasted about four days, five days, or a week sometimes, and then I'd be back drinking."

The worst lies are the ones we tell ourselves. Lying becomes the native language for addicts. It becomes a practice and sometimes an art. Frank lied to himself that he could stop drinking through Lent and through life.

Frank came up from the basement with his son to walk beside him in recovery and find his own. That was the immediate result. Further down the road—past the Road Closed section of highway—were trips to the Shepherd's House for Frank, a live-in shelter for the homeless addicted in Lexington, Kentucky. Residents are on the lowest rung of society's ladder far from picturesque horse farms, blueblood Lexington society, and others in the network of horse people in the self-proclaimed Horse Capital of the World.

He learned about addiction there, his own and that of others. Frank was never a resident at the Shepherd's House, but he led meetings there occasionally. One critical thing he learned, essential for recovery, is that addicts must separate from the old neighborhoods and haunts that fostered addiction.

Frank also learned something about himself: With his heart, soul, mind, spirit, and, yes, wealth, he wanted to give back. This translated into a response for Frank: "If I'm focused on helping somebody all the time, wanting to drink goes away for me." The first part of that statement—"I'm focused on helping somebody"—had been a priority in the life of his father, Joe Taylor.

There was also a business reason. You don't build a business the size of Taylor Made without ideas and creativity to go with hard work and savvy. The farm, like every other horse farm and entity in the Thoroughbred industry for that matter, was short on help.

"I already had the entrepreneurial idea," Frank said. That was a school of horsemanship, a ninety-day training program in horse care for new hires at Taylor Made Farm in the "art and science of Thoroughbred care."

The school uses a manual that distills everything there is to know about horse care in forty-four pages, created on a laptop and run off on a copier printer. It should be required reading for any individual working at either a horse farm or racetrack with Thoroughbreds, and rough-hewn though it may be, it is a masterpiece. Combined with daily hands-on experience it can ready an individual who has never touched a horse to successfully step into a job with Thoroughbreds.

The manual might be something of which Joe Taylor would be proud. It begins with a section that starts, as it should, with safety instructions—critical when working around one-thousand-plus-pound animals. For instance, horses should be approached from the side as they cannot see directly in front of or behind their bodies. Another instruction for staying safe might be the most important: reading the ears of a horse. Ears pinned back means agitation and is a warning that a bite or kick might be in the offing.

The section then shifts to horse health, presenting every product commonly used in hoof care, for example, and what a groom's kit should include.

The lifeblood of a horse farm like Taylor Made is breeding and foaling, and the second section is A to Z from what should happen in the breeding shed to signs and stages of foaling.

A much shorter third section on business knowledge prepares the residents for horse sales. Students learn to read horse pedigrees to assess the sales potential of a horse. Lastly, but equally important to pedigree (if not more so), is a comprehensive hoof-to-head review of the *conformation* of a horse, or how it is built. Things like the angle of a horse's shoulder can tell whether movement will be free and flowing for proper stride length and running efficiency.

Secretariat is often spoken of as having perfect conformation. Whether true or not is debatable. What isn't debatable is the fact that if he was perfect, he's the last horse that was. They all have flaws, some negligible and some overruling the most sparkling pedigree. An experienced bloodstock agent or trainer can look at a horse and see the potential for a specific injury. A trainer, in some cases, can develop a regimen to minimize that potential and buy a horse passed on by most buyers that will become an earner on the racetrack for a fraction of what a sounder-looking horse might have drawn in the sales ring.

The school and something far more important are an inheritance of sorts from Frank's father. Joe Taylor authored an acclaimed how-to book for building a horse farm and breeding and raising Thoroughbreds aimed at would-be farm owners and those already in the horse business. In its 314 pages the book spans everything from "Fences, Gates and Latches" to "Managing Employees" on a horse farm. It is, however, about more than horses.

Joe Taylor believed in taking a certain path in life, being grateful, and also giving back. The last paragraph in the final chapter, "Thoughts on Life as a Horseman," includes this advice:

> Make time . . . for doing charity or volunteer work or whatever is in your power to make this a better world. Be thankful for what God has given you and be at peace with what He has not. If you are kind to your horses and your family and grateful to God, you are a success already.

Intelligence and compassion obviously blended in Joe Taylor. His son Frank is the proverbial apple that didn't fall far from the tree.

Frank saw in the men he sat with in a circle of chairs at the Shepherd's House during meetings a potential source of labor . . . future students in the school of horsemanship.

He also saw a way to give back, a way, through the school and horses, that could meet a need that all of us have, but particularly those who have lost what most have never had: purpose. "Purposeful work" became watchwords for the idea that was to take shape in Frank Taylor's mind—not factory work or taking orders from behind a fast-food counter that is standard for addicts in recovery but work that put men in relationship with horses. Imparted would be a reason for getting out of bed in the morning and living each day as someone valuable. On another level, purposeful work could lead to a career if someone wanted it.

The school, however, was not enough. The men from the Shepherd's House came and went daily for work at the farm, but something was missing.

Frank had a light-bulb moment when he visited the Lexington restaurant DV8, founded and owned by Rob and Diane Perez. DV8 only employs recovering victims of substance abuse disorder. It is not a gimmick to parade human curiosities before customers or attract well-meaning folks wanting to help through their patronage. The Perezes share with Frank Taylor the same motivation: to give back and to help people who need it. Somehow, the Perezes knew, too, that recovering addicts, working together, can become a community of support.

Frank's idea, however, would go one better than DV8. He would apply that key principle he had learned at the Shepherd's House: The homeless need a community separate from the world where alcoholism and a substance abuse disorder had spawned. Taylor Made Farm is where that community would happen.

The idea would only become a reality after a review and sign-off with Frank's three brothers, obviously, stakeholders in whatever Frank had planned. They were not an automatic rubber stamp. Frank's reputation with his brothers was to ask forgiveness, not permission. His idea—bringing homeless men to the farm to work with the world's most expensive horses—was a big gamble on what sounded like another of Frank's typical plunges ahead on his own. Not surprisingly, the brothers needed convincing about this plan for solving a labor shortage. "What if somebody gets hurt?" "What if somebody overdoses and dies?" These were just two of the questions asked. Frank answered with a response that might have been what his late father would have said: "Yeah, but what if you save somebody's life and reunite a bunch of families?"

Business know-how and vision had to combine with negotiating skills and willingness to compromise. Frank knew his brothers first as family but also as business partners. A big project was going to be difficult to sell, especially one with the obvious risks involved with entrusting horses worth six and even seven figures to homeless addicts.

"I said, 'Just let me start small and the minute something goes wrong, I'll pull the plug on it.' I got them to commit to that little piece.

"We Taylors are very conservative, and we worry, looking at the downside a lot. It was easier to sell this for sixty days than it was for six months or a year."

Looking back over a little more than a year, Frank said "There's no doubt the formula works. I think it's about getting the right people in the right spot."

The first right person for Frank was a formerly homeless man who had found recovery and risen to vice president of the Shepherd's House, Christian Countzler. Christian confirmed the need for putting addicts and alcoholics into a safe, supportive environment.

He would also do far more with Frank Taylor.

4

Homelessness and Nights on a Riverbank

I just could not figure out why I couldn't figure it out.
—CHRISTIAN COUNTZLER

You would guess Christian Countzler was a football linebacker on some level, high school or college. His erect posture accents a brawny build. It is no surprise to learn he was a soldier in the U.S. Army's famed 101st Airborne Division. He is a veteran of the Iraq War.

Seven years ago, he probably weighed eighty to one hundred pounds less than he does now, and sickliness would make him even more unrecognizable to those who didn't know him back then. He had, in fact, *been* sick, spending thirty days in an Owensboro, Kentucky, hospital after a drug overdose. He was a methamphetamine addict and alcoholic.

The bed in his hospital room was the first he had slept in in years. A tent had been his home on the banks of the Ohio River at a park in Owensboro in what he termed a homeless camp. He slept on the ground with newspapers for a blanket. The floor of a porta potty sometimes provided respite from winter cold for a couple of hours when his tent wasn't enough on some especially bitter nights. When even the porta potty became too cold, nearby twenty-four-hour convenience stores or gas stations gave him temporary warmth until he was shooed out into the cold by an employee.

A drug overdose that hospitalized him was the beginning, finally, of rehabilitation from his drug addiction and alcoholism. Something about him touched the hearts of his doctor in the hospital and two nurses: They pooled money to buy Christian a bus ticket to Lexington, Kentucky. A staff member from Recovery Works Georgetown, just north of Lexington, would meet him at the bus station and drive him to this live-in treatment facility.

Many addictions start not with first-time drug use or a first alcoholic drink but with a wound. The drug or first beer or cocktail is a stealthy, covert balm or salve to that wound. The novelty of escape from pain that most addicts are unaware of is going to mean many more drugs and much more alcohol from that first encounter. It is remarkably similar in principle to an allergy but with a reaction that is the opposite of anything physically negative. Instead, there is a hyperreaction to a stimulus and relief from inner pain in the soul. It works for a time before it becomes deadly, betraying the addict after a dependency that makes "just say no" laughable. The betrayal is the control the addictive substance eventually exerts, eating away at the body and worse, the addict's or alcoholic's spirit. It is far more than an allergy but a disease of the heart and mind.

Christian's wound came from an alcoholic father who was physically abusive to his mother and emotionally abusive to him. "I grew up telling myself, 'I'm not going to be my dad,'" a resolution made by many children of alcoholics not realizing their wound harbors a disease that will mean almost instant susceptibility to drugs or alcohol. It is like a poison seed waiting for germination.

His grandmother, an English teacher, was the sole positive influence in his life, encouraging him as a student. Good grades helped him earn an ROTC scholarship at Western Kentucky University.

An introduction to cocaine at college was the first relief from pain for him. It also eventually got him kicked out of school after only three semesters. The Army and the Iraq War followed. If that didn't deepen the wound from his dad, it inflicted its own damage. He was a crew chief on Blackhawk helicopters ferrying the wounded, dying, and dead back to base. He saw humanity at its worst, killing and maiming.

The Army ended like his time in college: a bad-conduct discharge after he "caught a marijuana charge."

Returning to Muhlenberg County in western Kentucky, Christian married and fathered three daughters. The area was coal country, and he went to work as a miner to support his family. That job was where he began using a drug that may have done more damage than the cocaine that got him expelled from college or the marijuana that ended his time in the Army.

"My very first day underground, somebody walked up to me and stuck out his hand with some pills and said 'Man, you're going to need these.' Everybody was taking pills. It was during the OxyContin epidemic and I just kind of fell in love with it like everybody else."

Even with a drug-shortened college education and short-circuited military stint, opiates, for Christian, was where his life "really took a turn for the worst.

"For the longest time, I hid the fact that I was a junkie because I made enough money in the mines to have what we needed as a family. From the outside looking in, it looked like everything was okay, but I had a two-hundred-dollar-a-day habit with pills. I ended up losing my job in the mines. My wife left me and took the kids.

"I was so in the throes of my addiction that instead of thinking, 'Oh my God, I've lost my job, I've lost my wife, I've lost my kids,' all I could think about was 'Oh my God, I can finally drink and drug the way I've always wanted to.'"

The disease of addiction had grown to what could make it terminal for the sufferer. He was a slave to drugs and alcohol.

Several years before the bus to Recovery Works Georgetown, he met a young woman at a treatment facility in South Shore, Kentucky, and, once released, followed her back to her home in Lexington. "I ended up getting arrested two weeks into that and got extradited from Fayette County [Lexington] to Ohio County." After release from jail there, homelessness in Owensboro, Kentucky followed . . . three years of it.

Only those who have experienced it can fathom the physical and emotional poverty of homelessness. And only an addict can understand the complete power of drugs or alcohol to reign over and destroy one's life. *Alcoholics Anonymous: The Big Book* states simply and chillingly the path of addiction and the pull of a substance: *Many pursue it into the gates of insanity or death.*

The homeless camp at English Park in Owensboro took Christian to those gates.

Kentucky, like no other state in the contiguous United States, has the most distinct four seasons. This accounts for the same number of warm and cold days, ideal for aging the bourbon for which the state is famous but also for weather extremes. Summers are usually stifling. Winters can sometimes be severe, killing homeless men and women from exposure.

The porta potty that became necessary on particularly frigid winter nights may have saved Christian from death by exposure to cold.

Whatever the season, the days were all the same for Christian. "Your entire day is spent chasing alcohol and drugs and figuring out how you're going to make it that day."

Life itself is solely about those substances. And it is violent.

"You're fighting for territory. You're fighting for drugs. You're fighting just because you want to fight somebody that day," said Christian. "And you can't trust anybody.

"I cannot tell you how many nights I laid down in an abandoned house or on that riverbank, and as long as I had a spoonful of dope and a little bit of liquor, I was absolutely okay with my life. That's how bad and sick I had gotten. I didn't give a crap that I was sleeping on the banks of the Ohio River under a newspaper because I was going to be okay for the next couple of hours."

He had no answer for how his life had led to survival in the elements and an insatiable, gnawing appetite for drugs and alcohol. "It's different for each individual. For me, it was just this absolute abhorrence of myself. I hated the fact that my life had gotten to where it was and that I could not stop it. I could not stop drinking.

"I would go to treatment and have a bright outlook and within a day or two I'm at the liquor store and within a week, I'm back in the woods or sleeping on the riverbank. I just could not figure out why I couldn't figure it out."

The betrayal of an addictive substance replaced the honeymoon of pleasurable escape. Thoughts of a better life in the future and what had been, at times, a good life in the past, tortured Christian as it does many homeless men. That past is far back in the distance, obscured by an abject future and every second of a present that is a personal hell.

"You're just not capable of doing the things you need to for a normal life to happen. Every day is a struggle. You're just surviving."

The overdose that landed Christian in a hospital in Owensboro may have been a brush with death that led to a different gateway—an alternative to insanity or death that would lead to a new life.

It was in his time at Recovery Works Georgetown—the "tenth-plus" time in rehab "but never for the right reasons"—that Christian had a moment like the one Frank Taylor experienced in the basement of his home.

"I was either going to get sober or I was going to die, and I did not care which one of those happened. I was not going back to the streets. If I couldn't get sober, I was going to end it.

"I made this promise that I was going to give sobriety everything I had. I was going to put everything I learned in the military, every bit of what my grandparents taught me, into putting effort into my sobriety, and that's what I did."

That meant finding a live-in rehabilitation facility to follow Georgetown after twenty-eight days there.

"I started asking people, 'Hey, I want to stay sober. I need a place that's really going to help, and I need a place that's tough.' Almost unanimously, everybody said, 'You need to go to the Shepherd's House in Lexington.'

"It had some structure, which is what I do well with."

In addition to structure, it had something else that was essential: time. Residents, in a very limited sense, were prisoners, unable, ostensibly, to get to drugs or alcohol. "I had never been sober longer than thirty days in probably twenty years."

What Christian found at the Shepherd's House were four things: structure, discipline, accountability, and responsibility. These four words today are on a wall at a beautiful home for Stable Recovery (SR) residents on Taylor Made Farm, Preston House.

"I had numbed myself for so long that every emotion a typical, normal human being would feel, I had sedated, numbed, and avoided at all costs. Every single day it was something new that I had not done in twenty years. And that may have been as simple as having a feeling about something. I had to learn how to adjust to having feelings again."

Those four things from the Shepherd's House not only propelled Christian through the year he was a resident but also led him into recovery work as an administrator after a year free from drugs and alcohol.

He was the night house manager first at the Shepherd's House. He set schedules for household chores, held people accountable for those chores, checked curfews, and much more. It was the day-to-day that would give him experience he would bring to SR.

After that, a promotion to case manager put him with individual residents. He supervised their progress with their program (in addiction circles, the term for personal progress toward sobriety and recovery) while also coordinating necessary visits to doctors and other professionals.

Amazingly, a year after taking on that role, Christian became a vice president.

"I loved the Shepherd's House. It saved my life."

It also brought him into contact with Frank Taylor.

5

"Going Terrible" and the Turning Point

Well hell, let's do it.

—FRANK TAYLOR

The birth of Stable Recovery (SR) was six months after Frank Taylor spoke the words above to Christian Countzler and the purchase of the first house for program residents. The statement is "classic Frank Taylor," according to Christian. Indecision is something with which Frank may not have even a passing familiarity.

Christian recalled a Zoom meeting with Frank and the farm's chief financial officer on an idea—a school of horsemanship on the farm to train men and women in horse care. The idea was still embryonic but with one firm objective: to bring homeless addicts and alcoholics into the school. Frank had met with several organizations and was meeting with Christian when he was vice president of the Shepherd's House in Lexington. This facility would become the sole source for pupils in the school.

Christian remembered well his first meeting with Frank and his way of expressing himself. "He said, 'This is what I want to do. How do we make it happen?'" It drew Christian in.

The idea of a school and jobs for Shepherd's House residents had instant appeal to Christian. He knew something vitally important was missing from the Shepherd's House: *purposeful work* . . . the same thing Frank Taylor saw.

"My first job at the Shepherd's House was at a car wash. It was humiliating, and there were many days that the thought occurred, 'I'm not going,'" said Christian.

"I knew what it felt like to be a soldier. I knew what it felt like to be a coal miner. Both of those jobs had purpose. When you told somebody, 'Hey, I'm a coal miner,' you felt pride in that."

Behind the counter at Wendy's or on the floor of a factory is a paycheck. Nothing more. Christian felt strongly that a job with purpose—a job someone could feel good about—would help cement sobriety and recovery. "If you're not built for it, a nothing job is absolutely the right mix to cause a guy to relapse, no matter how well he's doing with his recovery program. If financial insecurity hits or depression comes from getting up every day and doing something you don't feel good about, you're risking relapse."

Christian had made it his role to go out and make connections with people and businesses in Lexington and the surrounding region, offering "second-chance" employment opportunities. Taylor Made and Frank Taylor's idea for a school of horsemanship were ideal, Christian thought. It meant training and then work that was purposeful.

Frank and Christian first met on the porch of the Shepherd's House when Frank brought a family member (not his son) to the house for rehabilitation. Christian had no idea who he was in the horse industry or the Lexington community. He did know, however, that there was a labor crisis on horse farms and that included Taylor Made.

Later, Christian would find himself in a meeting where Frank talked about his idea for the school. "I thought, 'Wow, that could be something special.'

"I hadn't been around horses yet, but I'd been around animals enough to know that there's just something about an animal that is completely reliant on you, that's completely loyal to you—that helps a man, especially a man suffering from trauma, substance abuse disorder, alcoholism, anxiety, and depression."

The first year of the school awakened Christian to possibilities beyond the Shepherd's House as a resource for Taylor Made Farm and
the nascent School of Horsemanship. "I would come home and think,
*Man, you need to dedicate an entire program to the school, Taylor Made
Farm, and the horses.*"

A huge part of Christian's interest in the school was what he saw in
Frank Taylor. "Frank was just one of those guys that genuinely wanted
to help people. You don't meet people like that. Most of them are doing it for a headline or to make themselves sleep better at night. From
the nastiest of the nasty, Frank would help bring guys back."

Christian began linking the Shepherd's House with Taylor Made
and the School of Horsemanship through coordination with the Kentucky Career Center (KCC) and the Fletcher Group. KCC is an adjunct of the Commonwealth of Kentucky's agency for helping the
unemployed find jobs. The Fletcher Group is a not-for-profit entity
founded in 2017 by a former Kentucky governor, Ernie Fletcher. It fo-
cuses on transitioning addicts from homelessness to "lives of hope,
dignity, and fulfillment," as the group's website states. The relationships of both KCC and the Fletcher Group to Frank Taylor and Christian were a first step toward making SR happen.

"There were months and months of Zoom calls through the Fletcher
Group, Kentucky Career Center, Taylor Made, and me at the Shepherd's House," said Christian. "There were many, many kinks that
needed to be worked out prior to guys being allowed on the farm: insurance, getting paid through the Kentucky Career Center, and much
more before implementation of any kind of plan."

One major kink was sign-off by Frank's brothers and other farm
executives to turning over the care of the most expensive horses on
the planet to, seemingly, the most unqualified people on the planet.

"Taylor Made was not quite sold on the idea," perhaps an understatement, "so I invited all the leaders to the Shepherd's House, and
I gave them my spiel: 'This is why we're different; this is why it will
work.' They were really impressed with the structure and discipline

and the way I did things at the Shepherd's House. It made them comfortable knowing these guys were not just wily drug addicts left to their own devices.

"You always enforce structure to set the direction of a rehabilitation program. That sealed the deal."

The presentation earned buy-in from Taylor Made, and Christian began sending men to the farm.

It was not to last.

The flow of men from the Shepherd's House went from steady to nonexistent after Christian left the Shepherd's House for another position.

"We lost something when Christian left there," said Frank. "We had twelve good graduates and then ten good graduates and then eight."

The solution for revitalizing and saving The School of Horsemanship was an easy one for Frank Taylor: Find and hire Christian. Frank found him managing a paint shop in Lexington, and his timing was dead-on. Christian was miserable in his job, and he had recognized fulfillment working with addicts. He felt like work in recovery was "God's path" for his life. He had thought about setting up a rehabilitation program of his own before hearing Frank say, "I want you to come work for me."

Looking back, Frank knows he couldn't have made a better choice. A familiar lament of his now, as he looks to the future of SR, is "I need 'more Christians.'"

Management of a rehabilitation home after thirteen months of sobriety was only part of what Christian brought to the table. He experienced what he knew the men of SR would need for recovery: community.

It would seem counterintuitive that the best person to help an addict or alcoholic is another addict or alcoholic, yet that is the formula for recovery, whether in a live-in facility like the Shepherd's House, N.A. (Narcotics Anonymous), or A.A.

"Experience, strength, and hope," famous watchwords of A.A., are what only an addict or alcoholic can share to help another sufferer. It really does *take one to know one.* Experience spans more than just knowing the path of addiction and enslavement. It can produce a built-in, acutely sensitive, and always-on bullshit detector in working with those in recovery.

Veterans of recovery know that those with a substance abuse disorder or alcohol addiction (or both) are typically expert liars, a skill they themselves developed when they were in their own addiction to hide their drug and/or alcohol use. It is a talent common if not guaranteed. There's an old saying in addiction recovery circles: "You can't con a con."

Thoroughbred trainer Will Walden, kicked out of the Shepherd's House by Christian during one of what Will estimates were eighteen attempts at recovery, is candid about why the nineteenth effort under the second supervision by Christian succeeded after his first banishment: "He called me out on my bullshit."

Christian credits what he learned while still in treatment at the Shepherd's House for showing him not only how to relate to addicts, but how to run a recovery program. The Big Book of A.A. states that half measures avail us nothing. This is probably the most famous truth put forth in A.A., and it is integral to the work and interrelations of SR.

"You don't have to drink or 'drug' to get kicked out of our program," said Christian. "If you're not pulling your weight, if you're not making the man next to you better, we don't need you here. That's the only way this works." A military background surfaced as he spoke, a fierceness coming into his countenance that has earned him this dead-on description from Will Walden: "He's a warpath alcoholic with a black belt in recovery."

Christian had fought the fight for recovery, ripping the bandages off wounds, exposing them to the healing light of a Higher Power, being accountable to others, and resurrecting long-suppressed feelings both good and bad.

"I got into being healthy again. I got into actually caring whether I could breathe or work out. Basically, any aspect of what I should have been doing for twenty years I had to relearn. It was like learning to walk again."

A phone call from Frank to Christian at the paint shop was a key event in the history of SR. Frank called to tell Christian things were "going terrible" with the school and seeking advice.

What Christian suggested was another component to complement purposeful work in SR: a common roof over the men.

"Frank, you gotta have a single program for housing where everybody is following the same rules."

Frank's response, in the history of SR, might represent a kind of five-word Declaration of Independence: "Well hell, let's do it."

Hummingbird Lane and the Preston House were to follow.

6

Hummingbird Lane and Preston House

We had five guys, and then we had no guys.
—CHRISTIAN COUNTZLER

There's an old saying: "Bad company corrupts good morals." It is so common a maxim that most would be surprised to find it is from the New Testament (1 Cor. 15:33). For the addict, it is more than a proverb or adage but applicable, inherently wise, and just plain common sense.

It was the principle behind the light-bulb moment Frank had when he visited the Lexington restaurant DV8. Most, but not all, employees there had homes they returned to after work.

While still at the Shelter House, Christian had advised Frank that Stable Recovery (SR) needed housing to bring residents under the same roof with common (as well as stringent) rules. That advice was the impetus for the "Well hell . . ." moment for Frank.

Frank instantly saw the wisdom. "You send a kid off or anybody for thirty days or ninety days, and they go learn some life skills and some A.A. steps. They get armed with that, and they come right back to the same situations where they're hanging out with the same old friends. The same old drug dealers are calling them."

Bad company corrupting good morals.

For Christian, he knew from experience in the Shepherd's House how critical it was for residents to live together.

"It was not an A.A. meeting. It was not my sponsor. It wasn't so much the staff or the program. It was the men I was with in that program that pushed me to get better and do better," he said of his time as a resident of the Shepherd's House before promotion into administrative roles.

A recovering addict will tell you it is one of the great mysteries of life that only a recovering addict can help an addict who admits he or she is powerless over the addiction: "We admitted we were powerless . . . that our lives had become unmanageable." That is the first step of the Twelve Steps of Alcoholics Anonymous. "We" and "our" are key words. A solitary journey is not the path for recovery. It is connection with a community.

Christian talked about how that connection for him worked in practical terms: "I ended up there in the Shepherd's House with other men who were absolutely motivated to change, and we pushed each other in the right direction. If I didn't feel like going to a meeting, my roommate would say, 'Bro, get up. We're going.' If he was screwing up with something in his life, I would pull him up. It just taught me so much about what community and brotherhood can do."

Taylor Made Farm would bring men together, for certain, but it would also provide a setting—a horse farm—that was a novel environment in addiction recovery.

The farm and SR would also reverse the standard model for work as a part of rehabilitation. "The program usually comes first, and everything else is kind of a supplement to that," explained Christian. "With Stable Recovery, the farm is a farm. It has to come first. You gotta be there and you gotta do things.

"You had to have a program that adapted to the farm and not a job that adapted to the program."

The work was not something where you could call in sick with the sniffles or not give a good effort. Animals need feeding and care seven days a week. There are no days off. Also, recovery work is not something to fill time, but to fill a *life*. It is important work, as important as the Twelve Steps of Alcoholic Anonymous, Morning Meditation meetings, check-ins with sponsors, and Twelve Step meetings.

Who was going to establish and manage the community was a no-brainer for Frank. He hired Christian after engaging in some delicate diplomacy and negotiations with his brothers, not to mention some personal investment.

"The way I hired Christian back, I wasn't going to go to my brothers and say, 'We need to bring in a guy that we need to pay a big salary to.' I've got enough money now, I hope, to where I don't really need it, so I just told them, 'I'll just pay him out of my salary for two years.' That was sellable."

Christian knew his first task was to immerse himself in the School of Horsemanship, already launched by Frank and staffed by many residents from the Shepherd's House. "I knew that I could not ask a man to do anything that I had not done or would not do." Christian spent the first two months in the school learning, performing, and perfecting horsemanship skills just like other students.

He credits his military background and upbringing for preparing him for the rigors of handling and caring for one-thousand-pound animals.

"I didn't have any experience with horses, but I had grown up in the country on my granddad's property and in the woods, so hard work and hard labor is something I enjoy. I'm super competitive so I wanted to be the best at mucking stalls and anything else."

Gullette Barn, behind a beautiful home—Preston House—perched on a hill at the end of a winding drive, was Christian's first workplace, just as it is now for SR residents.

"I started with a pitchfork. I was at Gullette on the broodmare side and did exactly what any guy does on a daily basis. You wake up; you bring the horses up; you feed, water, groom, and turn out; and you clean the barn."

The next step was the housing that Christian had suggested to Frank. Frank loaned Christian $15,000 to buy a house on Hummingbird Lane in downtown Lexington, near Rupp Arena, and to renovate and furnish it. "He wrote me a check right then and I was able to pay him back within two months," said Christian. With the house furnished and renovated for lodging for eight, the only thing missing was the men.

An Old Testament scripture states, "Despise not the day of small beginnings" (Zech. 4:10). The first twenty-four hours of SR and the house on Hummingbird Lane were *no* beginning.

"We were hoping to have eight guys," said Christian. "We had five guys show up on the first day and on the second day, not a single one of them had stayed."

Within a few days, however, eight residents did come to stay.

Meanwhile, Christian had moved into Preston House on the farm. "The idea was I was going to help renovate it and help turn it into an Airbnb," he said. At the same time, SR was up and running on Hummingbird Lane and needed space for more men.

This set the stage for the boldest idea Frank had yet presented to his brothers. He wanted to move overflow from Hummingbird Lane to the Preston House.

The first reaction to Frank's idea by his brothers was predictable and went along these lines with more colorful language probably excised: "Let me get this straight: You're turning over horse care to drug addicts and alcoholics, and now you want them to come live on the farm?!?"

Just as with Christian's salary, Frank's willingness to take responsibility and to lessen risk sealed the deal.

The key was to minimize concerns and objections by presenting SR as an experiment, and a small one at that.

"Small" was for sixty days, far more amenable to Frank's brothers than six months or a year.

A nonfinancial bottom line may have also been a factor in the brothers uniting behind SR. These were, after all, sons of Joe Taylor, who was a horseman but also a remarkable man who touched the lives of many who needed something. "He was always helping somebody," said Frank, repeating what his brother Duncan recounted, not often said about most of us. The three brothers—Duncan, senior Thoroughbred consultant; Ben, president of Taylor Made Stallions; and Mark, president and CEO of the farm—proved that they, too, like Frank and the proverbial apple, hadn't fallen far from the tree.

It is ironic that a book Joe Taylor had written, *Joe Taylor's Complete Guide to Breeding and Raising Racehorses,* has an instruction that is a voice from the grave to his sons, Christian Countzler, and all the people responsible for SR:

> Consider the opportunity you have in training people who will take their place in the industry and in society. Here is the chance to teach what never appears in books about bloodlines and breeding theories, about great horses, and great people, and about the honesty and courage that made them great. Explain . . . what makes a particular broodmare so valuable and your hopes for her offspring. Instruct them to shake hands and greet people by name. Talk about business, about ethics, about courtesy, and about commitment, and talk about why you love horses. You are molding people as much as you are training employees. Instill your values as well as your methods.

Ironically, SR residents primarily work with the broodmares Taylor mentioned.

In January of 2023, residents with ninety days of sobriety at Hummingbird Lane moved out to Preston House. This transition path is still in place. A waiting list of those wanting to become part of SR has existed from early in the program's history.

There is one primary and overarching qualification for admission: "This is for men that are truly trying to make a change," said Christian.

It is also the "toughest program around, " he added.

How tough? You have no idea.

7

Nobody's Leaving

I thought 6:00 only came once a day.
—UNIDENTIFIED ADDICT

The chapter title may sound as if Stable Recovery (SR) is like a
prison. Few prisons—minimum or medium security—have a
regimen like SR.

For starters, the wake-up time at Hummingbird Lane is half past 4
for a thirty-minute van ride out to Taylor Made Farm in time for the
Morning Meditation meeting. There they will join Preston House residents who "sleep in" until half past 5.

This is a time for everyone to take a minute or two (or three) to bare
their heart, their hope, their soul, and to vent an occasional rant. Meetings begin with a short reading from the Big Book of A.A. (*Alcoholics
Anonymous: The Big Book*). The meeting is approximately forty minutes
long, and it may be the most valuable forty minutes of the day.

Work starts at 7 a.m. sharp and ends at 4 p.m. Dinner, however, is
going to wait. Vans heading back into Lexington and Hummingbird
Lane will stop at any number of A.A. meetings throughout the city before finally arriving home. It's the same for Preston House residents: a
recovery meeting right after work before the men sit down to dinner.

The only break is a weekday off in the first ninety days at Hummingbird. This is to integrate residents into a world most of us take for

granted. Many have never obtained a Social Security card. The assignment to Hummingbird Lane will, in part, get them squared away with health and legal matters. Doctors and dentists, courts, and parole officers are close by in downtown Lexington. Christian calls this day off also necessary for adapting to the structure and discipline of SR.

"We have lots of 'stabilization,'" as he termed it, "that needs to take place with their mental health and their physical health. Then I want them to get into the Twelve Steps. That needs to be the most important thing, not the work out here but learning how to connect with something bigger than them. That is what will keep them sober."

Admission is as tough as that of any better-than-average university but on a smaller scale.

"I've got a waiting list that's twenty-five deep [at the time of writing] right now," he said, adding that an objective is to maintain it at that level. "Some of them on the list are guys that are in longer-term treatment centers that don't get out for another two or three months, and there's a good chance there's a bed for them. I've got a guy who's expecting a bed today, and we don't have any more room. That's the hardest part of my job."

The waiting list is far short of what it would be if not for one seemingly small sacrifice that apparently is too big for an astonishing percentage of applicants.

"'You're not going to have your cell phone,' is the first thing they're going to hear," Christian said. The response from an unimaginably high number is almost always the same, running along these lines: "I gotta have my cell phone. Thanks anyway."

For those willing to give up their phone, the welcome speech from Christian doesn't vary: "I tell them, I'm going to be on their ass. 'You're going to do exactly what I say, when I say it, to the best of your ability on a daily basis, or you don't get to stay here.' There cannot and won't be any misunderstanding or misinterpretation of probably everything said to the men."

Obviously.

Christian's toughness and discipline are extreme, to say the least, sometimes causing Frank Taylor to cringe at just how tough he can be. "He's got that military training and sometimes that's uncomfortable for me. He will jump in their asses and give them an ass-chewing like you've never heard. It might be putting a lot on those new guys, and he never has told me why he does it so harshly. It's brutal at times."

Frank added: "I think what he's really trying to do is test their willingness. If they're not willing and they're here just to half-ass it, he'd rather run them out of here quick. If you bring a bunch of guys in here who are half-assing it, it just spreads.

"We've seen several of them leave, but the next thing you know, in a month or two, they're back. When they come back, they're totally different."

It wouldn't be realistic to expect everyone to make it and for a variety of reasons. "We had one yesterday," said Christian. "We put a Weed Eater in his hands and in about an hour, he said, 'I'm not breaking my back for this.'

"He missed the entire purpose. It's not about weeding a fence row. It's about staying sober that day. Surrender.

"He ended up packing a garbage bag full of clothes and walking down the road. He's homeless. He had a chance to make ten dollars an hour and have a roof over his head. But that's addiction . . . it's nothing more than addiction.

"This program is not for everybody, and we see that every single day. We have guys that show up who thought they wanted to be around a horse until they get in the stall with a thousand-pound-plus animal and realize, *Nope. I'm not gonna do this.*

"There are others who are not done yet [with addiction]. If they're not, they won't spend time staying here.

"It's both the work and the program. It's a pretty good mix of that. The work is hard, but the program is even harder. We ask a lot from these guys."

It is difficult to profile who will make it and who won't. In the first place, you can't lump drug addicts and alcoholics together. Each has their own characteristics.

The only dynamic that is telling, Christian said, is age. "It's from thirty to thirty-nine and especially between thirty-five and thirty-nine; that's when a guy has really kind of had enough and is ready to come here. He's young enough to keep running but it hasn't got him anywhere and he realizes it." Christian was thirty-nine years old when sobriety and recovery finally took root in his heart and mind.

The number of times in rehab is somewhat of a barometer for success. The only constant is it takes multiple treatments—anywhere from two to twenty. "I would say four or five go-rounds with rehab is a fairly good average."

In comparison to other rehabilitation programs, Christian is justifiably proud of SR's low dropout rate. "Most of the guys who end up here are pretty much fed up with what life has given them. Does that mean that we don't have guys whose addiction takes them out? Absolutely. We do.

"None of these guys are forced to be here. They volunteer to do what they need to do to get their life right."

Just as sobriety for SR has been as high as 94 percent compared to a national average of 12 percent for live-in rehabilitation centers, it might also lead the nation in the percentage of men who leave the program and then return. *That* particular welcoming speech is harsh to the point of almost comical when recounted by Frank.

He shared one story:

"I saw a guy come back. He was humble, and he was ready. I was just wanting to love on him, pat him on the back, you know: 'I'm so glad to see you back.' He walks up to Christian after the meeting and Christian starts in. Whatever he said to Christian, the response was 'This is why you're drunk all the time! Get your shit together.' He laid out about ten things and ripped the guy a new asshole.

"I think it was probably the right thing for him. Is he ready this time? Christian is not going to come in and lie to him and manipulate him. That isn't going to happen."

The qualification, wanting to make a change, seems and sounds simple . . . for non-addicts. Many addicts and alcoholics—those not ready for recovery—may not realize that what they like is the *notion* of recovery. The actual work will tell the tale of the desire for it.

Christian rates SR as the toughest program he has seen, and he has seen more than a few as a patient in what he estimates at twenty treatment programs and also as an experienced program manager after achieving sobriety and recovery. "We push these guys harder than anybody. Six in the morning? There's nobody else in this town starting at six who does this. Then they're going out on this farm and working all day then coming back and doing a meeting."

A surprise to anyone studying SR or seeking admission into the program is that tenure is open-ended. "We have not put a time limit on it. We want someone to be as established and in as good a shape as they can be before they move out," Christian said.

"In my experience, it does not take much for a relapse to occur. No matter how much work you do in the year or eighteen months that you're here, let financial insecurity or a family death happen and you can throw all of that away really quickly.

"Each individual needs a different set of parameters and rules, and for certain guys, we can allow more. We try to keep it on the individual and see where they are mentally, spiritually, and physically.

"I would recommend at least twelve months," he said.

Frank Taylor's heart is evident when he talked about the length of time at Taylor Made: "We like to see these guys stay a year. Some of them may stay forever."

To learn about life at the Preston House is to understand why.

8

The Few. The Proud.
The Desperate.

There can't be two 'Christians,' right?
—ELIZABETH BECERRA, SR PROGRAM DIRECTOR

Christian Countzler would admit to being the bad cop at Stable Recovery (SR) . . . a hard-ass.

"Let's get real, he *is* a hard-ass," said Elizabeth Becerra.

Somebody also has to be a good cop, a role occupied by Elizabeth. As the program has grown, she has taken on much of the intake process—a key part of SR requiring sensitivity to motives with would-be residents.

Her beginnings were as an intern lightening the administrative load for Christian and being the first face of SR to newcomers.

"Beginnings," you'll note, is plural. Her introduction to SR began as it does for any other resident entering the program. Therein was a problem. She was not a resident with a substance abuse disorder or alcohol addiction but an intern. Apparently, not everyone on the SR staff got the memo.

That came to light when the then-director of the School of Horsemanship made a keen observation expressed in less than gracious terms as he watched Elizabeth pick the hooves of a horse: "You suck at this."

"I was like, 'I know. I'm so sorry,'" Elizabeth replied.

His next question, asked with the tact of a Marine drill sergeant, was "What are you doing here?"

When Elizabeth replied that she was an intern, the director bore in a little more with continued, shall we say, frankness: "I know that. But why are you interning if you're terrified of horses?"

She responded she was there to work with people not horses. It was an "aha" moment for her questioner.

Much to her credit, there were several other days in the barn for Elizabeth to endure before her real duty as an intern began.

Her first day at SR was an initiation of sorts akin to a nonswimmer thrown in the deep end of the pool . . . a pool filled with sharks. In this case, Thoroughbred broodmares.

To add to her apprehension, she had witnessed more than a few horses kick her uncle, a farrier, as well as others.

She wasn't alone.

The story is comical mainly because of the mare's response to not one but two scared-to-death rookies. "On my first day, I got thrown into a stall with one of the guys who's still in contact with the program today. He's the first guy that I met. He looks at me and says, 'I'm terrified of horses. I got here yesterday.'"

There would be no tutoring or handholding for Elizabeth. No supervision of any kind. "I'm like, 'Oh my God, this is *my* first day.'"

Her function with the men of SR began in that moment. "He started telling me his story." The broodmare they were to groom, meanwhile, was looking back and forth like a fan at a tennis match as Elizabeth talked to her fellow newbie.

The mare calmed down. Elizabeth believes the horse sensed she had two stressed people in her stall who were clueless about what to do. Looking back at this first encounter with a horse, Elizabeth could imagine what the horse was thinking: *Good grief. I gotta give them a break. I can't be stressed too. Two stressed humans are enough without adding me.*

Either recognizing the need for cooperation, impatient for hoof picking to begin (or both), the horse began picking up her hooves as if to say, "All right, you can keep talking, but would you two please get to my hooves?"

The school director played fear-monitor yet again with Elizabeth but in a different scenario. After she was filling her proper role, he asked her, "Are you not terrified being in a room full of felons?"

This time her response was an emphatic "No."

"I was charged with two felonies at a very young age and found out that they are very easy to get. It doesn't scare me to be in that room. They're trying to leave their felonies in the past."

Horses may require fearlessness at times and drug addicts and alcoholics the same to a lesser degree. Elizabeth's expectation and reality were vastly different.

"I went into Stable Recovery expecting angry people. They won me over very, very quickly, because they were vulnerable. They were willing to share everything.

"They've done things that would make most people feel like they were sitting with a monster. But they also shared their struggles with their own mental health and their self-esteem, the way that they were brought up, and changing their mentality."

The reality was that the men of SR needed help and it wouldn't be a short-term project. "It's a lot of work to put in, and this is in just the first few days. They're the most sick at the beginning of the program."

The men who stay with it progress probably more rapidly in the environment and in the company of the horses than a new non-SR Taylor Made employee without horse experience. The reward of Elizabeth's work comes relatively soon. It is the change she sees in the first three months after which the men transfer from Hummingbird Lane to the Preston House.

She sees men sober and in recovery excited about "getting a job, really getting excited about it, and getting their feet under them. Even things like getting a driver's license are a big, big event."

Elizabeth might fill a role akin to a racetrack groom who spends the most time with a horse and who knows that horse better than anyone.

She is, perhaps, closest to the men because she is the staff person most in contact with them.

SR is growing rapidly in scope and with it, administration that is not the best use of Christian Countzler's time nor his forte.

"Christian valued me when I knew how to do insurance paperwork, when I knew how to figure out documents and things like the probation and parole system. I've done this at one time or another," she said.

Christian, too, saw in Elizabeth a kindred spirit. "I'm willing to do whatever we're able to do to get a guy one more day," she said.

A key task as program director and maybe the most important, is, again, the intake process for men entering the program. The challenge to Elizabeth was learning on the fly because she had no résumé-worthy experience in addiction recovery.

Her lone experience, which proved valuable, was growing up with an addict in her family and witnessing this person's behavior for years. The individual had even, in a moment of emotional desperation, asked Elizabeth for help. Closeness was difficult for her, a victim of this addict's behavior along with other family members. Her best effort was to take the addict to A.A. meetings. While she may not have had *technical* experience with addicts and alcoholics, her family history touched her deeply. Christian would help fill in the experience gaps.

Elizabeth's best training for the intake process was watching Christian question men wanting to enter SR.

"What's this bloke trying to get out of it? Where's their mind in getting into this program? Are they that desperate? Are they willing to do anything and everything to live one more day sober?"

She said she learns something daily from Christian just by watching him. She adds, not defensively but thoughtfully, "But I make the process my own, because I'm still myself. There can't be two 'Christians,' right?"

Elizabeth is not conscious of how she smiles when talking about the men. She may have had to learn an intake process from Christian, but it would seem she was born with the same heart.

"My goal in life was always to help people," she said, adding that what that looked like changed over the years. A curricular "medical pathway" at Woodford County High School (which borders Lexington and Fayette County to the west) began her quest to help others. Her objective? To be a doctor specializing in OB-GYN (obstetrics and gynecology).

An internship with the University of Kentucky, where she would enroll after high school, put her in a hospital pediatric ward and a job that, to date, is the only one Elizabeth has ever quit.

"I could never imagine being in a hospital thinking these people are helping you, but in reality, they've already helped you as much as they can, and those are your last days. We were making them comfortable, and it sucked."

A teacher helped put her on a path that was a last stepping stone to SR. She had seen how Elizabeth took to community work and encouraged her to pursue it with the Woodford County Health Department.

"I finished out my internship just being like a facilities assistant. I helped everyone. I did environmental science. I did accounting. I worked with the director and did outreach." Community health education is where she found her niche, instituting a practice that is still in use in the county.

She is a second-generation Latina and daughter of Mexican parents who own a popular restaurant, Taqueria Becerra, in Versailles, Kentucky, the Woodford County seat.

Something she noticed right away was that only a small percentage of the Latino population in Woodford County took advantage of the free health clinics. Not surprisingly, the no-shows were undocumented Latinos who feared deportation if required to identify themselves at a clinic. This would not go overlooked by Elizabeth, who, because of the restaurant, was acquainted with most of the Latinos in the county, documented or otherwise.

"They [Woodford County Latinos] all watched me grow up, so you can't hide from me. I'm coming to get you. You're gonna get your blood pressure medication, you're gonna get your insulin. You're going to be healthy on my watch."

She went out to farms unannounced to take blood pressure, sometimes out in the fields. Other "Elizabeths" now follow this practice.

She employed the old proverb "If the mountain won't come to Muhammad, then Muhammad must go to the mountain." Her approach was successful, but Covid interrupted it and reduced her work to serving customers at her parents' restaurant.

A regular customer was Freddy Maggard, a well-known former quarterback of the University of Kentucky's football team, who undoubtedly saw an extraordinary young woman who might fit with a program that became SR.

One day, as Elizabeth served Maggard at the restaurant, he asked her first a question befitting SR's first School of Horsemanship director: "What are you doing?" The second question was more penetrating: "Where are you going with your life?" Maggard himself had an idea for her that was SR. He was a member of SR's first board and invited Elizabeth to come to some of the organizational meetings.

After finishing extra classes at UK she called him in November of 2023 to ask if SR might be looking for interns. He gave her a number that was Christian Countzler's.

"I called him and he said, 'Can you come in at seven tomorrow morning?'" Not knowing whether the meeting was for an interview or work, Elizabeth met Christian, who hired her on the spot. She started work the next day.

She saw immediately that SR was only for those who were at a point in their life and addiction where they had the gift of desperation.

"The ones that leave, leave within the first thirty days, normally within the first week."

Christian added that in the first seventy-two hours, they will lose three out of ten.

"If we can get them to the ninety days, that's when it jumps up to eight or nine out of ten making it."

Surprisingly, given that men begin right away working with horses, it is the program regimen and not the horses that causes them to quit. "Whenever I do an interview for a guy to come into the program, I make it sound like it's going to be the worst thing to ever happen to them. I want it to sound absolutely awful so that they know to expect something hard." Elizabeth said.

"I tell them the schedule: 'You're getting up at four-thirty. You're making your bed. You're going to the farm. You're attending Morning Meditation. You are then cleaning up afterwards. You go to the barn, you train, you work, and then you come home. You cook or help cook or help clean or do bookwork or you're meeting with a sponsor before a meeting, either one that we host or an outside meeting.'"

The day ends at around 9:00 each weekday night.

After her brief foray in the School of Horsemanship, residents would meet with Elizabeth if they had a need. The meetings were as beneficial to her as to the men.

She gleaned information on recovery and specifics like detox, for instance.

"I fell in love with these guys, the population in itself.

"My dad's an alcoholic. He's been sober for thirty-five years."

Hearing the men and her family history evoked the compassion and love that has to be a part of helping others with sobriety and recovery. "I saw my dad. I saw myself when it came to mental health. I saw someone's son, someone's brother, and although I knew everything that they had done to harm the people that they loved around them, this was an opportunity to help them understand how to have a healthy relationship while still figuring out for themselves how to grow as individuals.

"It was also the fact that maybe this is their last chance, that this could be what keeps them alive for one more day.

"Even after Stable Recovery is fifty years old, and we only have one guy that has twenty-five years of sobriety, that's huge, knowing that for twenty-five years, this guy was able to have a real life."

The men and the horses will change over time, but the "secret ingredient" to the program, as Frank Taylor describes it, is the other side of the coin opposite recovery work—the horses, in and of themselves instruments of recovery.

9

And Then There Are the Heroes

How many animals in this world will let you climb on their back and let you ride around? Horses were put here for a purpose, and I think it was to help us find God.

—CHRISTIAN COUNTZLER

Christian Countzler, Frank Taylor, and many of the men will tell you starting the day with a spiritual exercise doesn't end with the recitation of the Lord's Prayer that ends Morning Meditation meetings. It continues with something uplifting to the soul of each man fifteen minutes later. If "uplifting" sounds a bit over the top applied to what happens next, you're not an addict or alcoholic who needs a lift from the very bottom of life.

They have met with their Higher Power, but now they have another important encounter after they walk fifty yards up a gravel road from Preston House. It is, of course, with the horses. They are creatures of habit with internal clocks as regular as Big Ben. Their massive heads already hang over the top rail of fencing awaiting the men. They do this every morning. In the grand picture of all in this world that is beautiful, ugly, imperfect, perfect, tragic, serendipitous, this daily reunion is something full of simple love and peace.

It is a "God moment."

An anecdotal aside here:

Thoroughbreds arguably are the apotheosis of the species, with a carefully planned evolution that has sculpted them into spectacular beauty. "Ferraris on four hooves" is the best I can do in trying to describe their beauty. They look fast standing still. I freely admit that getting "literary arms" around the "something" outside of the horse that is good for the inside of a man, according to Winston Churchill, is as impossible as getting literal arms around one.

My introduction to Thoroughbreds came when I moved to Kentucky after graduating from college. I had the great good fortune to live in Lexington, home to the Keeneland Race Course.

I was a racing fan going to Keeneland before a love affair began with Thoroughbreds. I discovered the mysteries and challenges of past performances in the *Daily Racing Form* and handicapping—analyzing the "PPs" to predict and bet on results.

Keeneland was integral to the love affair. It is arguably America's most beautiful racetrack, with a stately, stone grandstand, pin oak trees shading paddocks, and the atmosphere one might expect from a fine old English race venue. The backdrop in the distance, past the back stretch of the racetrack, is gentle knolls and paddocks. To complete the picture, Thoroughbreds dot the landscape and graze in those paddocks. An artist couldn't envision and create a more beautiful tableau. Keeneland, quite simply, is out of a storybook.

It was the paddock at Keeneland where a *flirtation* with Thoroughbreds pushed the races and handicapping aside for me. These were the days back in the mid-'70s when a Wednesday crowd was six thousand or so and not the twenty-thousand-plus that flood it now. It was easy to walk from the paddock under the grandstand to always find a spot on the rail to watch a race and then return to the paddock.

I began, however, to stay in the paddock after watching the jockeys come out from their quarters to be legged up onto their mounts. I didn't want to lose my perch for the next group of horses to race. I had to see the horses and see them up close.

Love begins with physical attraction, and so it was with Thoroughbreds in that paddock. People with no inclination to see horse races but appreciate beauty should go to Keeneland one April or October day. One should spend time beside the area where horses walk among mature trees after coming from adjacent saddling stalls. Any first-timer should follow the horses from the saddling stalls after they are "tacked up," or saddled, and not leave before the jockeys come out for their mounts. Horse and rider then walk to a small circular paddock for a once-around before heading out to the track through a tunnel under the grandstand. No other sport—none—offers beauty like this. Thoroughbreds are the stars of a marvelous equine parade.

Somehow, in my job at the time as an advertising copywriter, I fell into writing magazine articles for one of the agency's clients. I also happened, at the time, to cadge copies of *Keeneland Magazine* from the mail room. There began the idea of writing about horses and horse racing, which took me from flirtation to *relationship*.

The magazine had just begun hiring freelance writers rather than writers from a sister publication. My timing was perfect.

It may have been my first assignment that took me to Keeneland, where I happened to be in the barn area one morning. While the physical attraction was there with Thoroughbreds, they were like the unattainable best-looking girl in the class. You're not going to get close, in this case and in my mind, because of danger. I believed a stereotype that all Thoroughbreds are fractious, high-strung, and not people-friendly.

A presumably unnamed colt, so young as to have only the sire and dam on his halter plate, walked away from a groom giving him a bath. To my surprise, this baby walked away toward me (which he was not supposed to do) with a look on his face not of *Ahh, somebody to bite* but simple interest in someone unfamiliar. I saw something in his eyes that seemed to ask, "Who are you? I haven't seen you before." He had the innocent, fearless inquisitiveness of a child, which he was in horse years, with the same childlike curiosity. I was smitten and have been ever since that moment.

Turf writing does not require proximity to horses, but I've intentionally put myself in and around barns and even held horses while they were being bathed. I've rubbed their noses as they stood in their stalls, and just recently I had one of the five greatest experiences of my writing life hotwalking a horse. I confessed in my story that every time I get around a Thoroughbred, I inevitably baby talk to them. It's ridiculous for a horse weighing a thousand pounds but impossible for me not to do.

One of my editors, Nick Godfrey, went for the idea I proposed. (May God richly bless Nick for approving it.) The horse I walked was a two-year-old colt named Salute the Stars.

Horses have a sense with humans that is amazing. I held a shank clipped to his halter as he got a bath before the walk, and I did my usual share of rubbing him and baby talk. I'll always believe the nudge he gave my arm with his nose when I stopped rubbing him briefly to talk to someone nearby was like him saying, "Hey, back to me. I'd like more of that rubbing." Life is full of small, unforgettable moments. At least as a writer and lover of Thoroughbred horses, this ranks in the top five.

Many of the men of SR get the same experience I did but daily. You don't need to wonder whether I'm envious.

"I watch the guys, and there's always mares there at the fence," said Frank Taylor, talking about the daily, morning reunion of men and horses after Morning Meditation. "You watch these new guys who have maybe never touched a horse before. The mares are hanging their head over the fence and the men are rubbing on them. There is definitely something about a horse that's good for a man."

Christian Countzler was a pioneer of SR by virtue of entering the School of Horsemanship before men from the Shepherd's House and other rehab centers. His quote opening this chapter is a beautiful expression of the value he believes is inherent in horses in general.

As for the Thoroughbreds at Taylor Made, there is a difference: "These aren't mom and dad's ponies in the backyard," said Christian. He appreciates the world they are born into and the role they may play. "These horses either came off the racetrack or are producing horses that will. Some are champions."

The relationships between the horses and the residents of SR are often discussed among the staff in quiet times, Christian said.

What is necessary for the men is recognition and acceptance of their need for help, and a willingness to seek it, to replace the substance of choice that no longer provides relief but only destruction. But who can they turn to for that help?

Christian believes God created horses for a purpose that dovetails with the need for addicts and alcoholics to come to believe in a *God of their understanding*, as the third step in the Twelve Steps states. Surrender, submission, capitulation—whatever you want to call it—to something "bigger than them" is essential, Christian believes. The horses are the source of help.

Christian said the men come to SR in several categories. "A lot of guys come into this program and are completely lost, especially when it comes to a Higher Power. Either they haven't met God, or they've shied away from God, or they absolutely resent God.

"Eventually, your security and reliance need to end up in God, who you can't see. Teaching these guys to place their security and reliance in a horse, which needs to be trusted, which needs to be fed, it's just tangible.

"The horse is also going to put his faith in you. They're counting on you to be at the gate at seven a.m."

Christian said you can see in just a couple of days the effect of the horses on a new resident. "I've seen color come back in the faces of some of the men."

Particularly touching is to see someone come into SR who is extremely fearful of horses but overcomes it (or perhaps more accurately, the horse overcomes it for him). He spoke of a new man "taking little baby steps when he had the shank in his hands, just scared to be around the horses.

"In two and a half weeks, he's built that trust, just like you have to build that trust with God or a Higher Power.

"You can see how the relationship is growing and changing, and he doesn't have that fear anymore. It's the definition of what we're teaching. Just get in there and know that if you do things for the horse, the horse is going to return the favor."

Recently, at the time of writing, Josh Franks, the lead instructor for the School of Horsemanship and the SR men in it, began assigning two or three horses to the same individual each day to create relationships. Josh called it a game changer as the men take pride in *their* horses.

Yes, they are their horses, but also, as Christian said, the horses are partners in helping men in the most important thing in the program: "In building a relationship with a Higher Power or God, the horses are the bridge."

If it seems and sounds like something completely spiritual . . . it is. And it isn't.

The results of the horse-human relationship are in a spiritual realm. The process, though, detailed in the next chapter, is also in a natural realm that is measurable and proven.

10

The Spiritual and the Science

Humans teach horses to back up. Horses teach humans to go forward.

—LEIF HALLBERG

Why, when a horse simply turned to look into the eyes of one man in Stable Recovery (SR), did he know heart, soul, and mind that everything was going to be all right in his life? Why did another SR resident come to believe that horses sensed his *un*brokenness—the refusal or inability to submit to something or someone outside himself—and communicate safety and trustworthiness never given to him by a human? Why would an SR graduate and assistant trainer now on the racetrack say that horses made him finally feel like he could be "in the moment" and not "ten miles in the future or ten miles in the past"?

Each of these men and others in Part 2 are witnesses to transformation, healing, wholeness, and more wrapped up in recovery from addiction that came through horses. Is it something in an intangible, spiritual realm that provides the connection every addict needs and hasn't gotten from humans? Yes and no.

The reasons may only be known by a Divine Creator, and probably more people who know horses believe that than don't. But research has explored the reality of the transformative power of horses and uncovered physiological changes that validate what, heretofore, was a complete mystery. Horses in the therapeutic arena are nothing new, particularly with children, but the impact on addiction in men is new ground, yielding remarkable and even amazing results.

The old nature versus nurture debate mirrors the question of spiritual versus science in looking at the power of horses with one major difference: The science with horse and human relationships supports the spiritual in many instances.

Leif Hallberg, in her book *Walking the Way of the Horse* (2008), wrote:

> Is it possible that due to our belief that horses are somehow connected to the Divine, when we enter into their energy space, we also enter into an altered state of consciousness? . . . [D]oes this altered state of consciousness allow human neurochemistry to adjust and change to make room for new thought patterns and ways of being? (p. 19)

Chapter 1 of the book you are currently reading begins with "Horses can hear a human's heartbeat from four feet away." Amazing enough, but another phenomenon accompanies it: Horses can cause the rhythms of a human, or *oscillations* that occur naturally in the heart, to synchronize with the horse.

A horse's heart will experience three oscillations in a minute if it is at ease. For humans who are in a quiet, restful state, it is six to seven. Yet somehow when a horse and a human come together, oscillations of the human heart reduce to three to match the horse. To add to the mystery of this phenomenon, this occurs only when the human is in a calm, attentive, and apprehension-free state. Researchers call it a "coherent" state. In it, a horse will typically approach the human, somehow knowing they are safe from harm. *Why* this happens physiologically is undetermined and is probably inexplicable scientifically. Researchers theorize that the larger electromagnetic field of a horse, due to their size, dominates the smaller electromagnetic field of a human. That doesn't explain why a human has to be in the coherent state (or at least attentive and in the present moment) for synchronization to occur, or how a larger electromagnetic field dominates a smaller field to produce this phenomenon. It won't happen if a human is fearful or negative. (More on this is in the Afterword.)

Another mystery is presented in the second sentence of Chapter 1: "They can also know what is *in* a human's heart." Confirmed? Of course, not. But it certainly seems that way.

More than a few researchers and experts in equine physiology have examined this very thing.

Dr. Ellen Gehrke, in a pilot study entitled "Horses and Humans Energetics: The Study of Heart Rate Variability (HRV) Between Horses and Humans," wrote that

> results could be interpreted to suggest that when in the presence of horses, some humans, in specific situations or interactions, may experience a sense of increased brain function and an influx of positive emotional states. (Self-published 2006; HeartMath, www.heartmath.org)

In an article published in the journal *Behavioral Sciences*, "Horse & Human Heart Rate Synchronization: What the Research Tells Us" (sagehillstables.com/blog, 2024), Dr. Ann Baldwin and colleagues Barbara Rector and Ann Alden found that there were physiological and behavioral benefits for people and horses during guided interactions at an assisted living residence (11:126, 2021). When a human pays mindful attention to a horse as they engage with it in an equine-assisted learning activity guided by an equine professional, the dominant heart rate variability or oscillation frequency of the human may begin to resonate with the horse. Dr. Gwen Donohoe, owner/manager of Sagehill Stables in Winnipeg, Manitoba, Canada, commenting on the article in the stable's website, wrote that HRV may "trigger the healing process . . . and help individuals learn how

to self-regulate their own heart rate to achieve . . . more positive feelings and state of mind."

Studying the lives of the men of SR, could sobriety and recovery
stem from interaction with horses who sense a need? That is conjec-
ture, but it is fact if you ask the men, as you will read about in Part 2.

Humans, of course, communicate to horses unconsciously, according to Hallberg:

> Horses can sense through the smallest of actions, body posture, smells,
> and tones of voice how the approaching human is doing emotionally
> and physically. They respond accordingly, either inviting the human
> into their space, or using cues to suggest that they are uncomfortable
> with that human in their space in the current mood or state that he or
> she might be in at the time. (para. 3)

Psychotherapists Dr. Adele von Rust McCormick and Dr. Marlena
Deborah McCormick echoed Hallberg's observations on *messages* in-
voluntarily sent to horses by humans in their book, *Horse Sense and
the Human Heart* (1997):

> We can't disguise our feelings from animals because we give off tell-
> ing cues. . . . Feelings bring out chemical changes, some of which
> result in release of pheromones. Animals smell our fear, anger, con-
> tentment, etc. . . . [W]e have to base our interaction on honesty, mu-
> tual respect, and compassion. If we don't, they'll know it and respond
> accordingly. (p. 23)

Relationships good and bad, however, between horse and human
are subject to change just as they are between humans. You will read
about one addict who, coming to work still drunk to the point of stum-
bling from the previous night, received an appropriate but not-so-nice
reception from a horse he had worked with before that morning. He
believes the horse sensed impairment in him.

The attitude of the human, communicated unconsciously with all of the smallest of things, dictates a mirroring response from the horse. As one of the residents you'll read about in Part 2 expressed it succinctly, "Happy groom, happy horse; pissed groom, pissed horse."

Responses, though, are not subject to some rigid predictability limited to happy or sad.

SR residents, in some of the chapters that follow, recount moments when a horse, in their estimation, sensed an emotional need and reached out with compassion. You will read about how one horse laid his head on the shoulder of a man who was experiencing depression. Unhappy man, compassionate horse.

Stereotypes, in sum, aren't applicable to horses, particularly Thoroughbreds, generally labeled as high-strung, aggressive, and even volatile. You will read about how one horse playfully teased a new resident, discerning his fearfulness, demolishing the stereotype that Thoroughbreds will always bully a human in whom they sense weakness.

The men of SR will tell you that most all of the horses want to serve and collaborate with them. They will, for example, be the first, perhaps surprisingly, to break the proverbial ice with a new human in their presence. If the right cues come from the human, the horse, one SR resident said, will put their head down signaling *Pet me. I trust you and you can trust me.* One legacy resident (someone who has successfully achieved a year of sobriety with demonstrated recovery) believes this is the moment when healing begins.

Mornings are especially stirring when relationships begin for another day. It sounds and seems small, but it is powerful in its message and connection between horse and human: Horses always, *always*, await the men along a paddock fence, ready for that first rub down their nose, scratch of their neck, or ruffling of their mane by a human. For the men, it may be the first time in their life that someone is glad to see them.

Horses, obviously, minister to our mind, heart, and soul to some degree. The horse's response to the men sets the stage for their relationship.

To state the obvious, horses are nonjudgmental, accepting us as we are. They can't know of any transgressions, offenses to people, crimes, or anything else. For the addict, there is no need for pretension or maintenance of a persona with a horse. Even then, acceptance of what a horse offers is not instantaneous.

Reprising what racehorse trainer Will Walden said from Chapter 2, "It may take a month, it may take two months, it may take four months, but there will come a day when that horse looks them in the eye, and they know they are accepted." The issue is not whether the horse will accept a human, but rather, will the human receive that acceptance. More than one man you will read about in Part 2 has experienced silent communication from the eyes of a horse. Hallberg writes that this fulfills the desire for "feeling seen."

> Many wear masks of protection and form layer upon layer between our "true" selves and the selves we portray to the world on a daily basis. . . . We desire that moment when a beloved horse looks over his shoulder and *sees* us. (p. 153)

In addition to the cues they give, such as lowering their heads for petting, horses offer one hugely impactful lesson to humans overlooked through millennia: Despite the fact that they are prey animals who choose, typically, flight over fight, they always move in one direction—forward.

To study and analyze this yields possibly a powerful lesson for living.

In Eckhart Tolle's book *The Power of Now* (1999), he introduces readers to the notion that "once in the present, we can move through crisis, pain, and suffering without getting stuck in those stages" (as cited in *Walking the Way of the Horse*, p. 23).

Hallberg offers a poignant example of how a mare manages grief over her baby colt or filly that has died to illustrate Tolle's point:

Once the baby is dead, the mother horse will stand for a time near the body but will re-join her herd and appear unfazed by the event within a short period of time. Life goes on, and she continues to trust her herd members . . . even though it was painful. (p. 22)

Humans by contrast, Hallberg wrote, would

prolong the moment until it is no longer a moment, but rather a lifetime of memories, pain, and suffering. . . . Horses constantly remind us that "forward" is the way to go, and if we can begin learning from their way, we can radically readjust our thinking about moving through trauma. . . . Horses can help remind us that the present is all we really have. (pp. 23–24)

Horses move forward to survive. Is the same true for humans and particularly addicts?

It is safe to say that addicts live in a mentality of regret for the past that constantly shadows what is going on in the present. Recovery, for at least one man in SR, meant experiencing an epiphany that "radically readjusted his thinking": the present—not the past nor future—is where he needed to live.

That "present" for the men of SR can be the communal life at the houses on Hummingbird Lane in Lexington and Preston House on Taylor Made Farm. "Can" is the operative word because thoughts of the past can haunt, and thoughts of the future can depress. Acceptance of love and collaboration isn't instantaneous with humans either.

Without realizing it, however, the relationship with horses can influence positively human-to-human relationships, particularly in a shared environment. One SR resident learned that horses really do have personalities, requiring adaptability in dealing with, say, a fractious young horse or a quiescent older mare no longer foaling babies. This man draws a parallel to human encounters, realizing that approaching every individual is a singular event best initiated with no preprogrammed expectations and, on his part, no standard template for communication and relationship.

Spiritual or science, nature or nurture, the Twelve Steps and Alcoholics Anonymous have one foot in each camp. Many believe alcoholics are born with a genetic predisposition to alcoholism. Others believe alcoholism connects to trauma. It is a moot argument; results are all that matters. The person with an experience—instant "allergic" reaction to alcohol or gradual capitulation to a craving to medicate trauma—is never at the mercy of an argument.

The men in SR, at least an overwhelming majority, would, however, line up with what Hallberg writes: "Horses become a source for connection to the Divine to many, and the barn becomes their church."

Truth or over-the-top falsehood? The stories of the men in Part 2 of this book will help you decide.

Frank Taylor, co-founder of Stable Recovery.

Christian Countzler, co-founder of Stable Recovery and president/CEO.

"Little Yellow House" on Hummingbird Lane, the first home for Stable Recovery.

Preston House on Taylor Made Farm and home to the School of Horsemanship graduates and those achieving ninety-day sobriety.

WinStar House on WinStar Farm in Midway, Kentucky, Stable Recovery's first satellite residence.

Taylor Made Farm barn.

Ken Snyder, author.

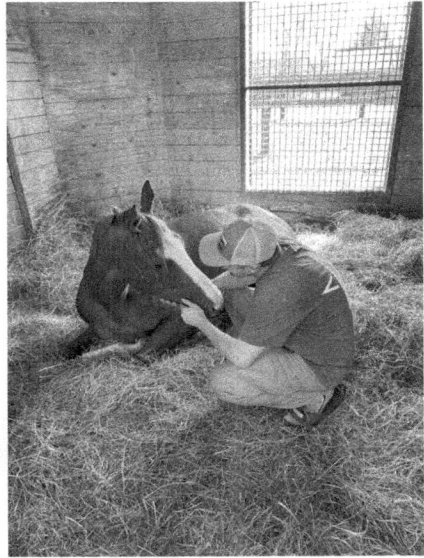

John Daugherty with a mare at WinStar.

Back in the stall . . .

Morning bath.

Mares in one of the many paddocks at Taylor Made Farm.

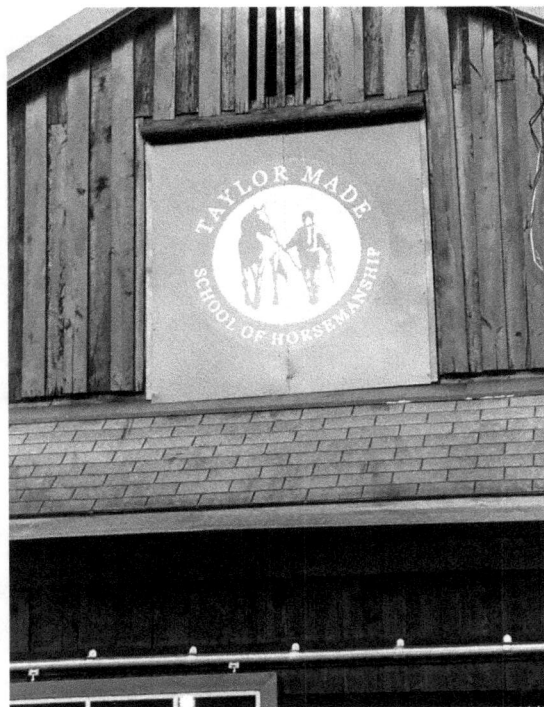

Sign on the Gullette barn, the School of Horsemanship's first home.

Gullette barn.

The view from inside Preston House.

Preston House in winter.

Paddock in winter.

WinStar barn interior.

Winter at Taylor Made.

Tyler Maxwell riding at WinStar Farm.

Tyler Maxwell at a stall door with a horse.

Coaxing a foal from momma.

Frank Taylor and Robert Osbourn
at an early Stable Recovery Gala.

Stable Recovery groom "tacking up" a horse at WinStar.

Three horses at the fence.

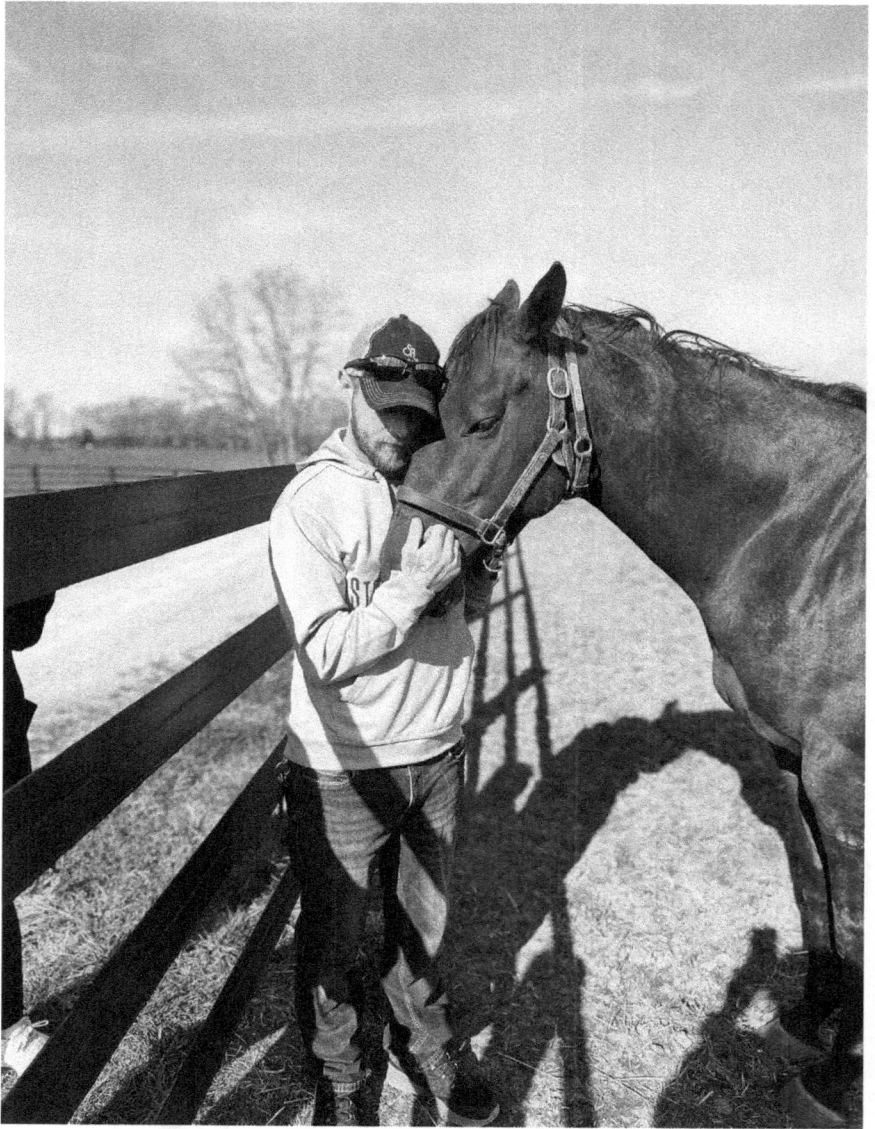

Stable Recovery resident and a horse have a "moment."

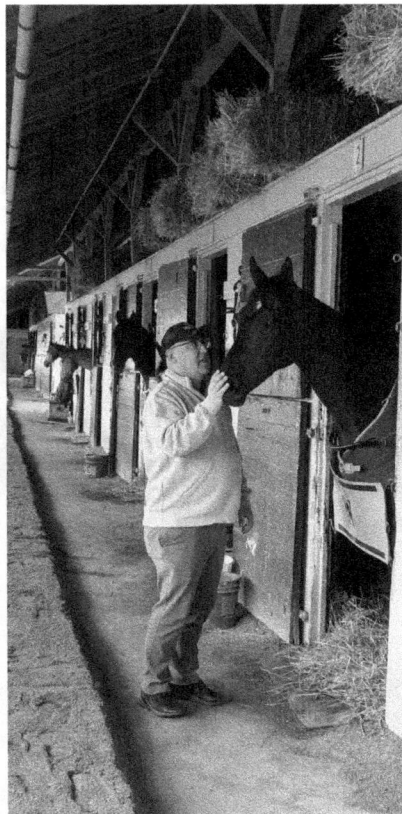

Will Walden in Keeneland paddock.

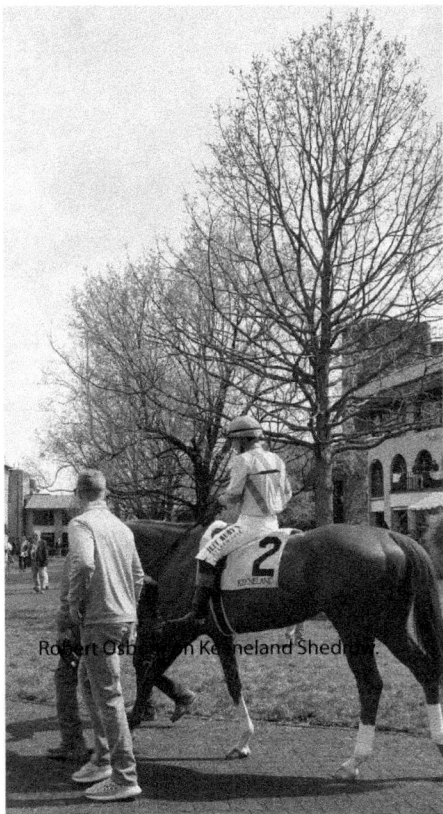

Robert Osbourn in the shed row.

The late Josh Bryan and mint julep cup.

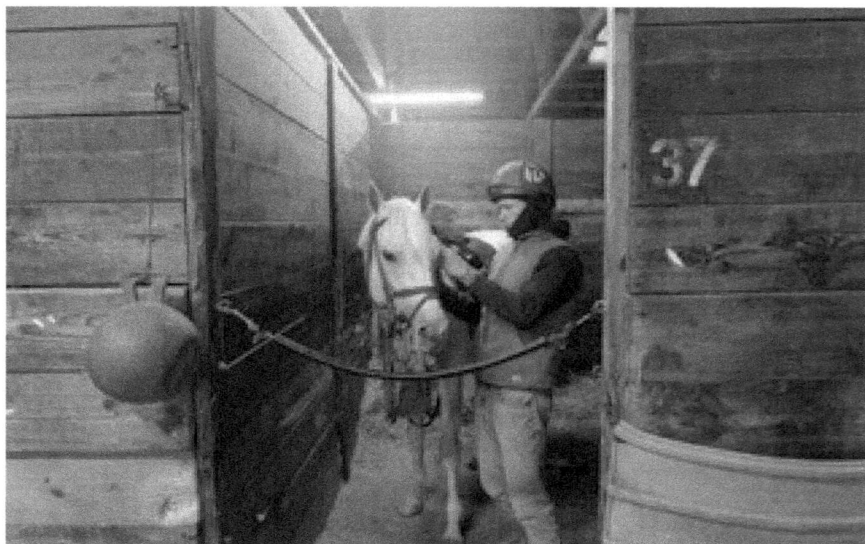

Will Walden tacking up a horse.

Josh Franks leading a horse to race.

Part 2

From Homeless to Horsemen

But what if you save somebody's life
and reunite a bunch of families?
—FRANK TAYLOR

11

"A Hand of Cards That I Could Finally Play"

I can tell if a guy is working the program by the relationship he has with the horse. The horse will tell me.

—JOSH FRANKS

I t is one of those early November mornings in central Kentucky where your heaviest fall jacket isn't enough and it is overkill to go with a winter coat. It's also early enough before daylight saving time ends that 7 a.m. is pitch black with only the slightest hint of a glow in the eastern horizon.

You hear the broodmares in one more of the seemingly countless paddocks at Taylor Made Farm before you see them. It may be surprising to those unfamiliar with Thoroughbreds and Thoroughbred life on a farm that they're turned out from barns as early as 10 a.m. and are out all night in the paddocks. The wide-open spaces and the horses' excellent night vision mean room to run at night over rolling topography. Running up knolls and rises in the land builds lungs. And run they will as they take flight between times of idle grazing. This is just one of many factors that make Kentucky the best land in America and the world for breeding and raising horses.

The men of Stable Recovery (SR) gather at the paddock gate on this morning as they do every morning, holding shanks—long leather straps with clips on one end—ready to attach them to a horse's halter and lead them inside to a barn stall. Only one man is inside the gate, Josh Franks, at time of writing the lead instructor for the School of Horsemanship. He rattles a small container of hard feed to let the *girls*, as he calls them, know breakfast is ready.

A rise in the middle of the paddock hides the horses, and as they run to the top of the rise, their silhouettes in the dimness of early morning on the horizon are unforgettable, unexpected, and dreamlike. One horse charges from the rise to the gate and to Josh, galloping over the dark ground, hooves thundering, kicking out hind legs in mid-gallop for the sheer joy of being a horse. It is a mama already feeling her oats before she can get to the real thing from a feed tub in the barn.

There's a reason for Josh to be alone inside the paddock fences and the residents of SR outside the paddock gate. Inexperience mixed with more than a pinch of fear keeps the residents behind the gate. A horse galloping at full speed in the dark will scare anyone except a person like Josh, who knows they can see him and won't run over him. He also can't wait for them to get to him. He loves them and is one of the naturals that Frank Taylor recognizes.

"My favorite time of the day here is feeding outside," said Josh. "I love watching these horses come across that field.

"I get it from guys all the time, 'Ain't you scared being inside the paddock?' I've never felt fear. Just seeing those horses running across the field, their manes flowing, their tails up—there's nothing like it in the world."

That absence of fear that put him inside the paddock is something Josh displayed from day one on the farm.

He can remember well the first stall he entered and the horse. "It was Big Lake, American Pharoah's son. I was with Will Walden." American Pharoah, for the non–horse racing follower, won racing's Triple Crown—Kentucky Derby, Preakness, and Belmont Stakes—in 2015.

"He had just worked out and had a bath and he had steam coming off of him. I remember Will telling me, 'It's ok, he won't hurt you.'"

Josh recounts the moment with a term he coined to describe the occasional times when man and horse draw near to each other by some invisible force: "It was 'match made.'"

"To touch these horses, for the animal to let me know it was okay, that's where the therapy is humongous."

The moment of trust between horse and man, when the horse didn't flinch or pull back when Josh reached out to rub the horse's nose, was wordless communication that confirmed what Will Walden had just told Josh: "He won't hurt you."

Hurt is something that has happened all too often in Josh's life. To know safety with a thousand-pound giant of an animal was indescribable for him. He shook his head in wonderment: He says again, "To touch these horses . . ." He cannot find the words to finish.

Some would say it was fate. Josh would say it was God's hand that brought him to this paddock and life on Taylor Made Farm. He loved horses before he ever touched one. During a ten-year stretch in a federal prison, one horse in particular consumed him. Her name was Zenyatta, winner of nineteen of her twenty races and purses totaling over an astounding $7 million. She was undefeated going into her twentieth race, the Breeders' Cup Classic in 2010, the highest-paying race in the U.S. annually and final race in a two-day "Super Bowl" of horse racing. It draws the best horses from all over the world.

Zenyatta got beat by a head, a characteristic late, always incredible, and, until now, always successful charge coming up just short.

"When she lost, I cried," said Josh.

Zenyatta put a dream in Josh's heart. He used to wonder, *How can I get around these horses? How can I get involved in something like this?*

During incarceration in Kentucky, initially for drug trafficking and two other felonies, he would routinely ask Latino inmates if they had worked with horses at farms in Lexington or on the racetrack. If they had, he couldn't get enough information about their work.

A second prison sentence of "two years and a day" was what addicts and alcoholics call his "bottom" and a time when "suicide was knocking on the door."

After release, he went to Recovery Works Georgetown, the same facility that was Christian Countzler's first step to recovery. That's where he heard about Taylor Made Farm and a program only two weeks old: Stable Recovery. Match made. Here was Josh's connection to horses and a dream come true.

"On day one I came in fired up about horses, wanting to learn, wanting to help. I was always in the staff's face, just wanting to be a part of something. I think they knew I was one who was really going to put in the effort here."

His enthusiasm and excitement earned him his own turnout after only two weeks when he moved from Gullette Barn, where all the new stable residents started, to "a little bit of everywhere" on Taylor Made Farm.

A friend he had made from Recovery Works, Mike Lowery, an SR resident who was part of Will Walden's race team, was preparing to leave Will's stable to come back to the farm for a job. When Lowery ran into Josh at the Preston House on the farm, he instantly thought of him as his replacement and told him, "I got a spot for you."

The two switched places—Josh going to the racetrack and Ready Made Racing, Mike Lowery going to the farm after training Josh for a couple of weeks. Progress for Josh was at the same warp speed as at the farm. He quickly advanced to barn foreman in Will's stable, working on the Kentucky circuit of racetracks—Ellis Park in Henderson, Keeneland, Churchill Downs, and Turfway Park across the Ohio River from Cincinnati.

If Josh had loved the horses from a distance, the racetrack only made it bloom.

It would take love to endure the hours and days that make time on the racetrack temporary for many people, including Josh. "We started at three-thirty or four in the morning, and we were usually done by ten, ten-thirty.

"We'd come back in at three in the afternoon to feed the horses and then we'd come back at night to feed as well. That night feeding was about seven or eight."

Time off? It was between those early morning, mid-afternoon, and evening feedings . . . seven days a week. There was no such thing as a *day* off.

It didn't take long for Josh to see something he sees often: horses seeming to know who has a need. "I got a guy right now who's come in here—tore, broken down—and I've seen a horse lay his head on his shoulder. It's amazing."

The love becomes reciprocal. "These recovery guys love these horses more than the average person, bar none," Josh said.

There is an order to how the relationship begins. "The horse approaches first. The human's always iffy.

"Usually, I'll have to walk a guy into a stall and get him comfortable, and the horses just come up with love.

"A horse will put their head down," a signal that they will let you touch them. "The horse is saying, 'I trust you.'" Josh marks that moment as the beginning of healing for the man who needs it. He called it "magical," something otherworldly that you can see but sense more than anything.

As lead instructor, most exciting for Josh is to watch a new man who, in his words, is "scared to death" experiencing that first contact.

"Once they overcome the fear, the confidence starts to set in. They start to feel good about themselves."

There is confidence, and then there is the courage to run your hand down the lower leg of a horse along a tendon, which causes the horse to reflexively lift their leg. You then lift the bottom half of the leg from the knee down high enough to get the hoof pointing straight up. You hold the leg with one hand while you pick the bottom of the hoof with a tool in the other hand that clears dirt, straw, and any small rocks.

It is, in all the care of a horse, the ultimate in self-accomplishment, according to Josh, and the acid test for overcoming fear. Legs and hooves, along with teeth, are the weapons of a horse. But once the men conquer fear, the personal bonds build between horse and man.

"They realize the horse isn't going to hurt them. You see more of the loving care after that."

Amazingly, the personality of some horses will dictate an initiation of a newbie and they recognize them right away. Josh remembers one horse, Soaring Bird, that would raise up one leg quickly with a newbie grooming them. "The person grooming would draw back thinking the horse was going to kick or something and you could see the horse kind of smiling. The horse just thought it was so funny."

That same horse would, when shanked to a hook or wall tie in the back of the stall, maneuver the shank clip somehow against the hook and slip his halter off.

"Usually, when they get out from a stall, they run. But he would sneak off really slow," said Josh with a laugh, describing how this half-ton horse tried to escape without notice.

They will also step on a hose as they're getting a bath to stop the water and playfully annoy those administering a bath.

They are like humans in that they have good days and bad. "I try to tell all these guys to learn their language. They're just like a human. Some days, they're 'Leave me alone. I don't want to be messed with today.'

"But as far as really, really aggressive, it's rare that we see that here."

A horse will talk most often with their ears, as experienced horsemen and horsewomen know, pinning them back against their head if they are angry, agitated, or ready to lash out.

"I had an incident in the barn not too long ago where two guys kind of went back and forth," recalled Josh. It had happened in the stall of Beyond Grace, the alpha mare of the herd. "She was up at the gate with her ears back. She was letting everyone know, 'Hey, I'm pissed. Don't let those guys back in the stall.'"

Not everybody makes it in SR. The work is as much a barometer of recovery as participation in meetings and relationships with other men in the program. "You're either going to get this thing or try to get it, or you're not," Josh said. Subjectivity is not part of assessing progress. There is no gray area between failure and success in recovery.

Surprisingly, fear is not what will cause men to wash out. There are plenty of jobs on a horse farm that don't require handling a horse.

Not everybody is there to recover. Josh can tell those who won't make it usually talk a lot about money. "They're going to make it in this industry, and this or that," a sign to Josh that they're neither going to make money, nor, more important, find sobriety and recovery.

"Guys serious about sobriety and recovery will show it in their work," he said. "A guy that's connected to God and is trying, he makes sure his horses have water. He makes sure their hooves are picked."

While the work is as much a part of the program as the Twelve Steps or recovery meetings, the horses cannot be the sole source for sobriety and recovery. Josh said he sees men making that mistake a lot, and it is something he has to remember in his own recovery journey. Twice in an interview, he said, "The horses can't be my recovery."

Helping men to recover is a war fought on several fronts. Josh tries, first of all, to pair men based on length of sobriety and personality types. While he said this is building "recovery momentum" in the resident's community and is working well, there are instances of personality clashes with a surprising solution. Christian Countzler will make sure two men in conflict with one another eat together, room together, and work together until they work things out. He reverts to Army barracks language to sum it up: "We'll shove them up each other's ass."

The second recovery tool is making sure a man is successful in his work, said Josh. "I got a guy, Chris, a special case for me who touches my heart to the core. He's probably the most nervous guy I've had around a horse. He's got a lot going on.

"With him, I had him do the same three or four horses, the easier ones in the barn, the ones I know that are laid back, the ones I know that love all the time. Then I tried to advance him to some more difficult horses. With him, I learned that was a bad move on my part. We went backward on that." Josh will guide him and bring him forward at a pace that will make success more likely.

The third and most adventurous aspect of the school for Josh is career development of the SR residents. "It's my job to find out what they're good at, utilize it, and build off that.

"I got a guy who's still nervous with the horses. But I noticed how particular he was with his meds for the horses, and how accountable he was with them.

"I do fake medicine charts with the men so they can learn, and some of the charts can be difficult. A vet may come in and say, 'Put this horse on Banamine for seven days, then switch to Dex [dexamethasone], starting it out on sixteen milligrams, drop it down to eight after three days, then step it down to four.' It gets tricky. I'll do practice med sheets to get them familiar with that and test them. This guy aces the tests.

"I'm thinking Rood and Riddle [an equine hospital] could really do good with this guy."

JOSH IS YOUR FIGURATIVE SR VALEDICTORIAN. IT WAS SHOCKING TO FIND out that at the time of writing he was just coming up on a year of sobriety. In his first six months, he had gone from beginner-hand in a racing stable to foreman in a matter of just weeks; gone from the beginner barn at Taylor Made Farm to assignments all over the farm in another two weeks; and soon after, lead instructor in the School of Horsemanship. He now manages a broodmare division at Taylor Made Farm. His desire in prison of "getting around horses" is more than met.

A deeply spiritual man, Josh credits his Higher Power—God—for every step. "He took my addiction and led me here," he told me.

It has been the unlikeliest of journeys. A single parent raised Josh, but the term "parent" is a complete misnomer. "I think it was embedded in my soul that I wanted a mother's love, and it was never there. My mom didn't know how to love.

"I never felt love before in my life. To be able to love a horse and have that horse love me back . . ." His voice trails off, and then he adds, "I never had parents tell me, 'Josh you can do this job' or uplift me in any way."

All he did know about his mom was that horses were her favorite animal and that she struggled with drug addiction. "She got addicted to pain pills and it ripped her life away and her sons as well," he said.

He knew less about his father, who was across the country in California. "I went back to California when I was fifteen or sixteen. My mom said she wanted me to experience my dad for what he was.

"He was a raging alcoholic. It hurt because he was taking care of a family out there and never had anything to do with me. I ended up doing cocaine."

His last memory of California was his dad chasing him around a truck to assault him.

"I caught a Greyhound and came back to Kentucky." Back home, a string of incarcerations began in 2012. "I was locked up for trafficking and making methamphetamine, and assault and burglary." This earned him a ten-year sentence.

A prison program, Residents Encountering Christ, and the program's three-day workshop were the beginning of a new path in his life. "To be completely honest, the only reason I went was for free brisket and coffee and candy. Sign me up.

"I went there, and it was the most powerful experience I ever had in my life."

He needed it for one final hurt from his mom. "My brother, she would let him stay there at her home but not me. It would break me down like a shotgun. I would sleep at the edge of the yard a lot of nights. It hurt me so bad. I'd had enough. I wanted something different in life."

"Different" began with meeting Mike Lowery at Recovery Works Georgetown and finding SR and Taylor Made Farm.

"When I got to Taylor Made, I knew the Taylor brothers' names before I ever set foot on the farm. I knew what year the farm started. I felt like I had arrived somewhere.

"It's really amazing. It's hard to put it into words. It fascinates me—the farm, the babies, the stallion names, the horses we work with.

"I felt like I was dealt a hand of cards that I could finally play."

12

"Stay Right Vertically and Everything Horizontally Will Be Okay"

I want to ride horses.

—TYLER MAXWELL

Major Thoroughbred horse farms in Kentucky have training tracks duplicating, on a smaller scale, racetracks. They are complete with inner and outer rails and the same surfaces for the horses to run on, even, in some cases, synthetic surfaces just like at public racetracks.

Watching horses in workouts might be as good as, if not better than, the races. Most usually, a daily workout will be a gallop, which is really a leg-stretching jog, one or two laps around the track. The second kind of workout is known as a breeze, spaced apart by at least a week and run at racing speed for a certain distance and timed with a stopwatch. A breeze is where it's found out whether a horse does or doesn't have the speed to compete . . . whether the horse is a *race*horse.

There are some conceivable but largely unpredictable factors in a horse's speed. The first is pedigree: how the sire (the dad) performed on the racetrack. The second is the performance of the mother (the dam). This gets attention even if the dam did not have a running record. The performance of the dam's sire can often be the truth-teller of possibilities. Conformation can be a factor, but mainly as a predictor of whether a horse will be subject to injury.

Pedigree and conformation combine for a pre-career assessment of value at sales. It's a complete shot in the dark. Yearling colts and fillies (between one and two years old) can sell for millions of dollars, but there's no guarantee of success on the racetrack. In 2023, two three-year-old runners, both costing $35,000—a pittance in the rarified air of Thoroughbred sales where million-dollar horse buys are common—won races at two of the pinnacles of the sport, the Kentucky Derby and Belmont Stakes.

The least predictable but maybe most crucial factor is the great intangible: heart. This can come with both inexpensive horses (see above) and million-dollar investments. It manifests in this innate desire in some horses to take issue with any other horse passing them down the stretch to that wire suspended over the track.

On a sunny but very gusty February morning I watched two horses gallop a short distance on the training track at WinStar Farm. The gallop was to stretch their legs, a prelude to a breeze over three-eighths of a mile. As they came at a gallop to a one-eighth-mile post where timing would begin, the two riders "sat down," as it's called, crouching low on their horse's back, head even with that of their horse, back perfectly horizontal. The horses knew from training that was the signal to begin running full-out.

In the matchup, neither pulled away from the other. There was a marked difference, however. The horse on the inside seemed to float, his hooves skimming the surface. Those in horse racing call this gait, or action, "cutting daisies." It is desired in racehorses because it is the most efficient method of running and the fastest. (It also can't be taught. Horses either run that way or not.) The horse on the outside, however, was not as smooth. He was keeping up, but with his hooves coming up higher, his neck bobbing much more than his running partner's.

I've spent hundreds of hours watching horses work out and I prefer it to afternoon races. I don't pretend to know a lot about what I'm watching or seeing. The farm trainer—a counterpart to trainers on the racetrack—watched closely with binoculars.

After the pair flashed past the post marking the finish, I saw an opportunity to ask the trainer what I figured was probably a dumb question.

"The horse on the inside seemed to be going much easier than the one on the outside. Was I seeing things?"

The reply was a relief for me: "No." The exercise rider on the inside horse had held back a bit on his mount to run with the other horse, to push the "busier" horse in hopes of improvement.

"That horse on the inside is an old pro who's had some success on the track," he added.

The old pro's rider was Tyler Maxwell, a former resident of Lexington's Shepherd's House and also former exercise rider for Ready Made Racing. Frank Taylor financed this stable, staffed by recovering addicts and alcoholics, most from Stable Recovery (SR).

The somewhat diminutive Tyler, five feet, eight inches in height and weighing 140 pounds, has the classic build for an exercise rider . . . compact and light. (Jockeys weigh anywhere from 114 pounds down, by the way.)

The journey from Tramadol, the first of many other drugs for Tyler, to trimming daisies aboard a racehorse on a billion-dollar farm is a long one, beginning when he was twelve years old and ending at age twenty-six. But even before age twelve, circumstances and events for addiction were in place. Both parents were teenagers when Tyler was born, and they divorced when he was two. He grew up in Bowling Green, Kentucky, where he said he bounced back and forth between the two parents after their divorce. "My dad would get custody one year; my mom would take back custody the next year."

Family from both sides bombarded Tyler with opinions and assessments of which parent Tyler should live with permanently. The tug-of-war alienated Tyler from both. "I never was close to either one of them," he said—not surprising given that both were flawed and, in the eyes of both sets of in-laws toward each other, awful people.

Tyler felt like he never belonged to either parent. "Growing up there was something missing," he said, adding the novel and subtly powerful metaphor, "I was basically a hole in the doughnut."

His grandmother Ruby, his mom's mom, took care of Tyler when his own mom "was still young and going out and doing thi[ngs, and not really paying attention." Tyler described his grandmother as a saint. If he belonged to anyone, it was her, and that was short-lived. "One day she had cancer. The next day she didn't know who I was. A week after that she was gone.

"That right there calloused my heart," he said.

A medical emergency, a ruptured appendix when Tyler was twelve, was the step that pushed him down the path of addiction that may have begun with the death of his grandmother.

"I had emergency surgery and I remember for about a month they had me on these pills. At the time, I didn't know what they were.

"I remember when I was taking them, it was not only fixing my physical pain, but everything else seemed to fall into place too."

The sudden passing of his grandmother, who had doted on Tyler, thrust him into adolescence more alone than ever and open to negative feelings about himself. This is typical for emotionally abused children and future addicts, who blame themselves for circumstances that they had no part in creating.

"It was like I woke up and didn't like being me," Tyler said.

Not surprisingly, middle school put him among what he called the "outcast crowd" who used drugs. Then began a detour from life.

"It was a journey that led back to the cabinets of my family where they kept their medicine.

"My seventh-grade year I remember I came home one day from school, and I went into my grandfather's cabinet—my grandfather Joe, my dad's dad—and I saw there must have been nine hundred Tramadol, fifty-milligram pills. Very seldom did he ever take them." (Tramadol is an opioid pain medication.)

"From seventh-grade year to sophomore in high school it was four or five a day for that many years." The availability of Tramadol stopped when his grandfather finally noticed someone was taking them.

"From there, it was Lortabs from my grandmother, my dad's mother." (This drug contains hydrocodone and is also an opioid pain medication.)

"Ten-plus years" of Lortabs, according to Tyler, followed the years of Tramadol. The grandmother would even give Tyler Lortabs as well as money. "She was very gullible, and I could manipulate her into anything," he said.

After graduating from high school, he went to stay with members of his dad's family in Tucson, Arizona, on a small ranch that he had visited before. Those trips gave him his first experience with a horse.

Tyler had expectations that, away from the Lortabs back in Bowling Green, things might be different.

"I took me with me," he said. "Nothing really changed. It actually got worse out there. I got introduced to cocaine and ended up losing a good-paying job.

"My dad ended up flying out there and driving me in my truck home." Tyler had only been in Tucson ninety days, "if that."

A job with a pest control company in Bowling Green was part of a series of near-death driving experiences.

"They started letting me take the work truck home. I had some routes I had to finish up on the weekends. One day I took a handful of . . . I'm pretty sure it was Lortabs.

"I OD'd.

"I remember I'd gotten to the stoplight, and it turned red, and I stopped. The next thing, I woke up in a ditch on the other side of the road just sitting there in this field."

Tyler told emergency medical personnel he had heart problems, which required him to go to a cardiologist in Bowling Green.

"They drug tested me, and I remember my mom was with me.

"The doctor pulled me aside and said, 'Look, I didn't want to do this in front of your mom, but this "x, y, z" is in your system and that's obviously not normal. If you need help, it's available to you.'" Tyler's response was an offhanded "Nah."

"That was the first time, at age eighteen, anybody had said, 'You need help.'"

He went back to the pest control company and driving privileges before losing this job.

"I wasn't being honest with my routes and the customers."

A factory job followed that paid well, enabling him to get a nice apartment in downtown Bowling Green.

Recalling the doctor's offering for help, Tyler felt he was "managing."

The beginning of the end was a friend's wedding and a DUI afterward that landed him in jail.

"Dad was there the next morning with my grandfather to get me out.

"Any normal human being would have put the brakes on," he said, but he continued getting high and working factory jobs after getting his driver's license back.

"At that point, my family started figuring things out," he said. Evicted from his apartment, he rotated between his mother's house, his sister's couch, and his grandmother's home.

"I hit the wall in my mom's living room. I remember telling them, 'I'm the one that's been taking your pills.'

"They knew for a few years that it was me."

For the first time, Tyler sought help at a place called Liberty Ranch in the mountains of eastern Kentucky.

"You'd get lost trying to find that place and you'd get lost trying to leave," he said.

He was there twenty-nine days. "They were trying to get me to extend my stay—to commit to a full year, but they didn't take insurance, only cash." The tab for thirty days alone was $3,200. Multiplied by twelve, it was too much money to ask from his family.

Addicts stay in addiction because they are enabled, and such was the case with Tyler. Incredibly, when he got home from Liberty Ranch and complained that his back was hurting, his grandmother produced a Lortab for him to take.

"I don't know what she was thinking. I can't explain it," he said.

"She never understood who I actually was and who we are as alcoholics and addicts.

"The only thing my family knows today is there's something different with me. It doesn't matter what it is as long as it isn't drugs and alcohol."

Despite going back to drug use—"the same routine, just different drugs"—he credits Liberty Ranch with planting a seed for sobriety and recovery.

"The only problem was my tolerance had gotten way too high. I was taking way too much.

"It just got to the point I knew my family's script dates [for prescription refills] better than I knew their birthdates. That's how I lived, and in between scripts it was even harder drugs.

"My tolerance was just ignorant."

He realized with fentanyl use, and his high tolerance of that extremely powerful opioid, that "something had to give. If this isn't going to do it, what is?

"I started thinking what is the 'magic ticket'? I wondered what the right milligram would be—how much I would have to take to die. It wasn't fun anymore."

In 2020 his stepfather helped him get a job. "This was my final straw," Tyler said.

It was the second time his stepfather had helped him get a job.

Again, he was making good money and bought what he called a "yeehaw" truck. This time his drug was Suboxone, a narcotic medication used to, ironically, treat opioid addiction.

True to form, Tyler lost the second job. The pressure was on to get another job because of truck payments.

Tyler is personable, and, on appearance and congeniality, you would figure him as a bright, up-and-coming young man with potential. He interviewed for a job at a bottling plant near Bowling Green and got a job offer.

"Instead of going home to my mom's house where I was living at the time, I stopped at a buddy's house to celebrate."

A case of beer led to a bottle of bourbon, then Tyler fished a bottle of moonshine from underneath his truck's seat. "We were sitting at the table playing cards, and I thought it was a good idea to break up a Xanax and put it in a blunt [marijuana joint] and smoke it.

"I somehow found the keys to my truck and was driving around Bowling Green and ended up rolling my truck at sixty-five miles per hour and being ejected. I came to in a hospital bed, handcuffed hands and feet to the bed."

From the hospital he woke up in jail the next morning.

A sense of helplessness and plenty of time to think about it was, against all odds, his turning point. This was his "bottom," inevitable for any recovering addict.

In jail for several months, strangely, Tyler felt like he "could actually breathe.

"I wasn't mad I wasn't going back to a job. I wasn't mad that I'd wrecked my truck. I wasn't mad that I was in jail. I wasn't mad that the ACL [anterior cruciate ligament] in my knee was torn. I wasn't mad at any of those things.

"What I was mad about was how I was still alive."

Released on house arrest, he continued to use drugs despite monthly drug testing over four or five months while awaiting a hearing on charges of aggravated DUI, criminal mischief, and first-degree wanton endangerment. At that hearing, something very unusual, maybe predestined in the heavens, occurred. Tyler's case was the last one on the docket and the judge, strangely, cleared everyone out of the courtroom before calling him forward.

It is, perhaps, meaningful that Tyler remembers the judge addressing him as "son." The words that followed were equally meaningful
and memorable: "'You have a problem. Either you can do something
about it, or I'll do something about it.'

"I said, 'All right.' I knew right then and there I was done."

He took a second stab at rehabilitation at another center in eastern Kentucky, Stepworks in London.

"I hated it. I hated treatment. I don't do well in treatment. I don't
do well with authority," said Tyler, adding, "I don't do well with other
guys and their emotions and attitudes that are exactly like mine."

Things, though, were about to change.

"They had mentioned Shepherd's House," he said, the facility in
Lexington that was an integral part of Frank Taylor's School of Horsemanship and SR.

He "did well" with the SR guys, entering relationships with fellow residents at the house "that were the closest thing he had to God."

These relationships included Thoroughbred trainer and recovering
addict Will Walden and Mike Lowery, who would be part of Walden's
Ready Made Racing stable and later Taylor Made Farm.

"All three of us were at the end of our rope," said Tyler.

A key moment for him was a meeting with Christian Countzler, who then was director of the Shepherd's House. He routinely
interviewed new residents to go over problems, progress, and all
other issues.

"I remember Christian asking me what I wanted to do.

"I don't know where this idea came from, but I said, 'I want to ride
horses for a living.' It just popped into my mind. I still to this day
have no idea where it came from. I'd ridden a few horses that were
already broke just for fun as a hobby—trail rides and stuff like that—
but I was in Lexington, Kentucky, and it fit with the environment.
Christian said, 'Okay.'" The next question dealt with the immediate
future for Tyler.

"He asked me, 'What *don't* you want to do?' And I said, 'Do not send me to a factory.'"

With a laugh, Tyler recalled working the next ninety days in a factory.

Tyler had also met a relative of Frank Taylor at the Shepherd's House and went with him for Thanksgiving dinner at Frank's home. The farm was still using residents of the Shepherd's House for positions on the farm, and he hired Tyler.

About a month before Will Walden, Mike Lowery, and Tyler were to graduate from the Shepherd's House, Will had the idea to start a racing stable. "Will promised me at the Shepherd's House he would get me on some horses, and he fulfilled that promise."

As with his arrival at the Shepherd's House, Tyler's emotions about going to Florida with Will and Mike were completely negative, but for a different and powerful reason. "I hated them . . . I hated them because they wouldn't let me quit. That's love." Tears stop him from going further.

In Florida the threesome attended A.A. meetings despite the long hours and seven days a week that racehorses require. A man named Randy came alongside Tyler when he asked for help in a meeting.

"He saw the willingness in my eyes."

Many recovering addicts believe that while all of the Twelve Steps of Alcoholics Anonymous are valuable, getting past the first three to brave the sometimes emotionally tortuous self-examination of Step 4 is a main key to recovery: *[We] made a searching and fearless moral inventory of ourselves.*

"I got some things out I didn't get out with my sponsor at the Shepherd's House," said Tyler.

For many addicts, recovery takes root imperceptibly. Not so for Tyler Maxwell: "One day I woke up, and it wasn't about me anymore."

Strangely perhaps, the awakening touched another area of his life. "I was able to really learn how to be on the backs of horses.

"I woke up one day and I realized the reason why I was alive, the reason why I went through all that pain. I went through the Shepherd's House to help somebody else. That motive right there answered my question when I was sitting in jail miserable . . . why I was still alive." He stopped to cry before repeating a benefit of jail time. "I was able to breathe, and I was able to actually think. Mike and Will and all they had done—I had love in my heart for the first time for those guys, for these horses. Then I was able . . ." Tears stop him again before a simple utterance: "These horses give me purpose.

"Stay right vertically and everything horizontally will be okay," said Tyler. "If I'm not right vertically with God, I'm not going to be right with them, the horses. They're not going to allow anything if I don't put what's first, first.

"They can't speak but they say it all."

This spiritual connection, love, and dedication to the horses he mounts each day explain how, according to Will Walden, Tyler learned in one year as an exercise rider what takes three years normally.

Talking about yearlings, it's easy to hear the deep, deep connection he has with them. "They look at you for that guidance how I look to God for guidance.

"They give me purpose because I know I'm doing my job. I know at the end of the day, I'm keeping the horse safe and I'm benefiting that horse.

"I don't just ride around the track with these horses. I get them to love what they do.

"Now I'm here at WinStar Farm riding million-dollar horses on a billion-dollar farm and it's all God."

13

The Gift of Desperation

*It may not happen all the time, but say you're having
a bad day. You're muckin' a stall, and you're kind
of zoned out. A horse will put their head on your
shoulder.*

—ROBERT OSBOURN

I t was another day of coming in drunk and/or high from the night before for Robert Osbourn, another day of pulling into a barn at Taylor Made Farm in a taxi.

Walking a horse out into a paddock, he stumbled and "kind of
bumped" into the horse's shoulder. "He bumped me back. When I
straightened up, I bumped him a little harder. Then he bumped *me* a
little harder. And then I hit him a little harder than he had hit me. That's
when he knocked me to the ground."

Robert Osbourn would tell you this was a classic tit-for-tat exchange
between horse and human. He would also tell you it didn't surprise him,
given his knowledge of and experience with horses and the wordless dialogue that is constant between horse and human. The horse was sending a clear message: *Don't come out here drunk or high. Have your shit
together if you're going to walk me.*

Robert has an interesting theory on why horses help recovering addicts beyond not taking any guff or sloppy inattention, accidental or

otherwise. "Horses are broken. You have to break a horse to ride, feed, and train it.

"I think all of us are broken and they sense that," said Robert. In the case of the shoulder bumping, it might have been classic "tough love" administered by a horse . . . *Don't make me your victim of what you're doing to yourself.* That's what Robert would tell you.

THE PROCESS OF BREAKING, MORE ACCURATELY CALLED "JOINING UP" TODAY by many horsemen and horsewomen, is introducing and familiarizing a horse with a saddle and rider. It has a parallel in addiction recovery. Horses must submit in accepting saddle and rider; addicts have to submit, period. This encompasses, essentially, the first three steps of the Twelve Steps of Alcoholics Anonymous: admitting that life is unmanageable; accepting and believing that there is a power "greater than ourselves" (something to which the addict can and should submit); and following through by turning will and life over to the care of that greater power.

Horses are fight-or-flight animals. Their instinct is to flee from a saddle and rider when introduced for the first time. These are new in a horse's mind, something that might not be safe. Through patience, experience, and expertise by good horsemen and horsewomen, horses learn otherwise, in particular they learn that the rider is trustworthy. In principle, the horse submits.

Frank Taylor uses the term "joining up" rather than "breaking" because it communicates entering into a trust relationship between horse and human. The starting gate is not some cage from which a horse will never escape. The floor of a horse trailer is not a trap door to a bottomless pit. A bit in their mouth is not an instrument to strangle or suffocate them. Horses, in short, learn to trust in the humans that introduce these things to them.

The first stage of a horse joining up with a human is when the human first lies across the horse's back with both legs on one side. The horse doesn't understand why a human is suddenly putting their weight on their back; all the horse knows in time is that the human is not there to hurt them. The next step is with legs on both sides of the horse's back. That's a tad more invasive, more so than just the weight across their back, and not as easily accepted. Sometimes they accept it the first time, and sometimes it takes a few times, but eventually it becomes permanent. Nothing bad has happened. The horse can keep trusting that human and other humans to be on their back.

Horses are also creatures of habit—feed at the same time every day; regular exercise gallops and workouts; daily baths on the racetrack—sometimes before saddling prior to a workout and a second bath after a workout—all predictable, routine, everyday events involving humans that they have learned are safe.

Thoroughbreds in Kentucky are arguably the most pampered animals in the world. Handling begins thirty minutes after birth and that is intentional. Someone walks foals to a paddock with one hand over their side and the other on their chest. This is not to prevent them from running away but to get them familiar with human touch. Humans will be with them in some form or fashion every day. Horses need to know that humans are safe. Yes, there are abusers of horses, just as there are parents who abuse children, but Thoroughbreds on Taylor Made Farm and most farms in Kentucky's Bluegrass Region receive the best feed, the best personal care, and the greatest attention. They are worth a lot of money, but they are also worthy of love.

In a certain sense horses discover, through joining up, submission. It is entirely possible that the reason horses are sensitive to addicts is that they see in them a refusal to submit, to trust, to believe that every person and every situation won't bring them harm. Maybe that is why the horses reach out, to communicate to addicts *It's okay. You are safe with me.* The benefits for the addict are structure and humility that break the chains of slavery to a substance. Mental clarity, reasoning and logic, the love of a horse, and a better life follow.

"THEY JUST WANT YOUR LOVE," ROBERT SAID. THAT IS, OF COURSE, IF YOU DON'T bump them when you're drunk.

At the same time, they love back. "They sense what you need," he said, reading and discerning what he calls "stall energy."

"Very simply, they can tell if you're happy or sad.

"It may not happen all the time. Say you're having a bad day and you're muckin' a stall, and you're kind of zoned out; a horse will put their head on your shoulder to comfort you."

He added with a smile, "They will play with you, just with you walking around. It's hard to explain.

"It's all about how quickly you become comfortable around them. Some people pick it up in a day. Some people might take a little longer. But I'd say it took me a couple of weeks. It's different when you're sober too."

Recovery from substance addiction demands submission, a foreign and novel experience for addicts. In many, if not most cases with addicts, someone in authority—someone to whom submission should be safe—a parent, priest, or relative—isn't. An invisible window falls between the victim and the world. They spectate but don't participate in life. The isolation is painful and only forgotten through temporary escape made possible through drugs, alcohol, or sex. In adults and children, in particular, they deduce that if they weren't a bad person, there wouldn't be imprisonment or isolation behind the invisible window. In childhood and adulthood, deeply embedded is the belief that they are damaged goods and unlovable, hence the virtual removal from others and the world. How can they be a part of the world when they are *less than*?

In the mind of an addict, the next fix or drink is the most important thing in life; no one is trustworthy, no one can love them, and no one will take care of them but them. Nothing moves the addict off these beliefs until they acknowledge that the substance used to medicate is simply a symptom . . . there is a cause behind it.

The fortunate among addicts see that they need help, and that self-help won't provide it. Self-help is a close relative to self-will for a drug addict or alcoholic. A Higher Power is necessary, something outside the addict able to shatter the window the addict lives behind. As the wife of one recovering addict said, "It's a matter of who's going to sit on the throne of your life—you or God." This statement parallels Step 3 of the Twelve Steps of Alcoholics Anonymous: *[We] made a decision to turn our will and our lives over to the care of God as we understood him.*

There's an old saying in A.A., repeated elsewhere in this book, that the program is really only two steps: Step 1, stop drinking or "drugging"; and Step 2, let God change everything about your life. In other words, the solution is easy, but the work involved is hard, and it's going to have to involve other people—Stable Recovery (SR) residents—and miraculously, the horses.

There is no straight line to either drinking cessation or changing everything about your life. Everyone goes at their own pace, generally loses sobriety after early success, and, if they're fortunate, gets the "gift of desperation," as Robert Osbourn experienced.

The spiral down to the need for that gift began when Robert's father, a successful and prosperous businessman in Lexington, committed suicide when Robert was fifteen years old.

"About six months before he died, he had a heart attack. I think that shot him into a depression that went untreated. Seeing someone for help about depression wasn't up his alley, and it just kind of grabbed him," said Robert.

For the survivor, suicide miscarries grief, aborting final acceptance of how and why the person could do what they did. We all can understand disease and car wrecks. We can't understand despair that is a private, personal hell for someone who believes death is their only escape. It is incomprehensible for those left behind.

"I was raised in an upper-middle class environment and enabled a lot. A lot of people felt bad for me," said Robert, but "they wouldn't do anything. They wouldn't say anything."

It should be no surprise and no coincidence that the one person who wouldn't stay silent or do nothing was Frank Taylor. Even though Robert had met him only once or twice at church, Frank came to Robert's house at 3:00 in the morning, just hours after hearing of the suicide, to drive him to the Perpetual Adoration Chapel at the Cathedral of Christ the King in Lexington to pray with him. The chapel would figure into Robert's life more than just this one time and was the site of a major turning point a few years later.

Processing his dad's death was one thing. A bigger challenge was answering the question, Who is Robert?

Drinking. Smoking marijuana. Pills. All obstructed the answer. The first few times Robert drank he had the temporary euphoria of feeling that he had "arrived." The destination reached, however, was a life completely off the rails.

Frank tried to be there for Robert with a real estate venture. "We bought an apartment complex," Robert recounted. "I fixed it up and did a good job with that when I was at the University of Kentucky.

"I started renting it out and it probably wasn't in the best location. I kind of turned it into a trap house and people were buying and selling drugs out of there." (A trap house, by definition, is a den for illicit drug trafficking.)

Frank's next effort with Robert was to bring him to the farm to work under a gentleman who was a recovering alcoholic. "That was a disaster," Robert said, referring to days of coming in still drunk or high from the night before at Taylor Made, like the one that got him bumped to the ground.

His performance or lack thereof got him fired and he moved to Alabama to live with family. Things there got off to a rough start when, in the second week, he drank to the point of blacking out—losing memory of things done while intoxicated. He learned later he had stolen a handful of pain pills from his grandfather. He woke up in jail. "I'd broken into some workout facility and shredded it. I couldn't remember a thing."

Robert escaped prison time and stayed five years in Alabama. In those years, he said, he "started doing better," although he was drinking.

He was sober from alcohol the summer of 2018 after moving back to Lexington, where he was earning money mowing grass, but admitted to "sneaking around smoking weed."

Doing electrical work at Lexington's airport followed, but his addiction also followed—prescription meds, alcohol, and cocaine. "I was in control," Robert said with a laugh.

An injury at work moved him to selling cars for a living, a job at which he was miserable.

"I was driving around one evening and had been on a four- or five-day bender and it just hit me: *I need help and I'm willing to do anything that it will take to get it.*

"I'd broken my phone because I thought 'they' were following me. It was a Tuesday night." That was significant. A Tuesday night was the night of his father's suicide.

He drove to the Adoration Chapel knowing Frank Taylor would be there at a certain time.

"I went there at seven-thirty and waited for him to come out. I came up on him in the parking lot and told him, 'I need help. I don't know what to do.'"

Soon after, Frank took Robert with him to Gulfstream Park in Florida and the stable of Ready Made Racing, the racing operation Frank launched to get Will Walden started as a racetrack trainer.

"I met Will Walden, Mike Lowery, and Tyler Maxwell," said Robert.

"I learned that Frank had bought these horses for Will to train. I'd see these guys every morning living the dream."

The impact on Robert of seeing three sober addicts was almost immediate: "Oh my God, I want what they have." Addicts will tell you that recognizing the possibility of sobriety and recovery in others and the freedom and peace they bring is a giant step.

Robert came back from Florida with the Ready Made crew for the annual April spring meet at Keeneland Race Course in Lexington. He then entered a program for addicts at an outpatient treatment facility and lived in a sober living home (a peer-managed house for addicts and alcoholics).

"While I was in treatment, Frank would call me about every morning to ask, 'When you comin' back to work?'" The calls, in retrospect, were caring, very touching, and classic Frank Taylor. Someone in Robert Osbourn's life was not just safe but accepting of him and showing him that he was worthy of love. The racetrack was important for Robert because it put him with men who had experienced SR. (At the time of writing, every stable hand in Ready Made Racing is a recovering addict.)

Robert remembers well his first workday at Keeneland with Ready Made: "I helped unload horses. We were there at three thirty in the morning, mucking stalls. It was fun. I'd been sober three months."

Working on the racetrack is fun but temporary for many people, particularly those with a family. Stables are at one racetrack for a month or a few months, then on to another track in another locale. It is not the ideal scenario for a recovering addict.

"I didn't like being away from Lexington. The track life was wearing on me. Seven days a week . . ." He shakes his head at the memory.

Even though he was faithfully attending A.A. meetings and was part of Ready Made's Morning Meditation meeting at the racetrack, Robert didn't feel like traveling and began to think a nomadic lifestyle was not good for his sobriety.

"I ended up coming back to Lexington. I was going to take a thirty-day rest, relax, and head back to the track."

Mike Lowery, foreman in the Ready Made barn, had become his sponsor while Robert was on the racetrack.

At the time, only a small handful of men lived in the Preston House, including Christian Countzler. At the house one day, Christian invited Robert to move in.

"Two days in, I couldn't sit still so I found a van for Stable Recovery to use." He began driving men daily from the Hummingbird House in downtown Lexington for work at Taylor Made and back when work was over.

"I liked it, and I enjoyed giving back.

"I saw how much potential this thing had."

Frank's involvement, Robert knew, would put him in proximity to Frank. "I love being around him."

He remembered one day when he told Christian his long-term plan was to go back to the racetrack. "He kept smiling at me. He said, 'I think you're going to stay here longer than that.'"

That came about through something that threatened the SR program and launched Robert in a direction that did, indeed, keep him at Preston House.

"Things were going good. The Kentucky Career Center was paying all our guys." (The KCC is an adjunct of the Commonwealth of Kentucky's unemployment assistance program.)

"I see Christian in the driveway, and he looks like he's seen a ghost. He said, 'The Career Center pulled the rug out from under us.'

"There goes the pay. These guys aren't going to work for free out here." That was the bottom line for the program and possible demise.

"I don't think we had much money at all in the bank."

At this moment with Christian, Robert had an epiphany: "Something hit me in that driveway. I didn't tell Christian, but I saw my purpose here.

"I'm not the best recovery coach, but I know a lot of rich people. I knew if I could show what I see going on every day, they're going to fund this thing."

That might be an understatement. The most recent fundraising golf tournament, an annual event, netted over $430,000 in 2024, a marked increase from $300,000 in 2023 and $90,000 in 2022. Additionally, the state awarded a sizeable grant to SR through the efforts of a grant committee headed by Robert.

"Purposeful work" is a mantra of sorts for SR. In the case of Robert Osbourn, he takes no credit for his own purposeful work. "I didn't do it. Frank didn't do it. Christian didn't do it.

"God is running the show.

"I love to do a little self-will when I get to feeling good about myself, but God does a good job of putting the lip chain on," he said, referring to a chain to maintain control of an unruly horse. In only one year and eleven months of sobriety at the time of writing, Robert has gone from angrily bumping a horse to using the metaphor of a restraint tool to describe how far he has come. Ironically, a lip chain is for horses who might run away.

To this day, Frank and Robert meet every Tuesday at Adoration Chapel.

There is no running away.

14

A Kind Eye

I know that look on someone's face when they have peace.

—MIKE LOWERY

Oh, if we could all have a life-changing moment like that experienced by Mike Lowery . . . without the circumstances leading up to it.

Three months into his work at Taylor Made Farm, in the early days of the School of Horsemanship, Mike was miserable, a state of mind that was nothing new for him. "I hated my life based on decisions I'd made in the past.

"I went in a stall one day with this mare and I was grooming her, and she just looked over at me. The way she looked at me with a *kind eye* told me everything was going to be all right. I got goose bumps. Right *now*, I got goose bumps," he said, as he recounted the moment. It was more than Mike's imagination. There was something he not only saw but felt in his heart, and he knew it was real.

"It freaked me out," he said. It also gave him peace. He knew right then he was where he was supposed to be—on this mammoth horse farm—doing what he was supposed to be doing, and most important, being with horses. "I decided right then to give this thing my all and make it work.

"I just really started grinding my ass off and just hustling."

Grinding and hustling was quite a change, to understate it considerably, from homelessness and nights sleeping in the outdoors in Lexington's Woodland Park not far from the University of Kentucky campus.

A drug addiction that had him, in his words, "shooting anything up" put him in that park. But strange as it may sound, there was an upside that can come from any addict's proverbial bottom. Mike stopped to look at things and think.

"I had found myself doing things that I said I would never do as far as shooting heroin or smoking crack. If I was just snorting it, I wouldn't have a problem, but the minute I started shooting up and started smoking crack . . ." His voice trailed off.

The root for the addiction was what he simply called discontentment, part of the trinity of woes that afflict alcoholics: irritable, restless, and discontented.

"I grew up in a single-parent household in the projects raised by my mother.

"We weren't dirt poor, but I saw all my friends with their fathers, and when I got older, I turned to the streets for validation and father figures." Thus began recreational drug use that was to become serious in short order.

Mike, who is thirty-three at the time of writing, made a first attempt at getting sober in 2017 in a treatment center. In the span of four years, there were twelve more times in and out of other centers, all unsuccessful.

He said the failures pushed what little bit of family he had away. They stopped checking on him. "There was no such thing as a friend," he said. "It just got to the point, nothing else mattered but getting high. Even sleeping outside was okay."

An interim step toward sobriety and recovery began with going to the Shepherd's House in Lexington, the same in-house treatment facility directed by Christian Countzler and home to several men who would become Stable Recovery (SR) residents.

"My mom had been reaching out to Christian for years and years before I actually went to the program he was running. When he finally met me, he cut me no slack. That's what I needed."

Mike had shown a "pretty decent work ethic" at DV8, the restaurant in Lexington that employs recovering addicts and gave Frank Taylor the idea for hiring addicts for Taylor Made Farm for the School of Horsemanship.

Christian Countzler approached Mike and three other men about a pilot program at the farm.

"DV8 was a great place, but I wasn't getting enough money, so I said, 'Let's give it a try.'"

Frank Taylor remembers well the first class of Shepherd's House recruits, which included two other residents who would go on to careers with Thoroughbred horses like Mike. "They had little horse experience, but they were superstars," according to Frank. "Mike was one of the best. He was a natural and he'd never touched a horse."

Mike somehow masked borderline terror with the horses, putting on a good front of fearlessness. This was for a full three months of being on the farm. "Hell yeah, I was afraid. A full-grown mare is twelve, thirteen, one thousand four hundred pounds."

The moment of looking into the kind eye of a horse was a wordless message to him to trust the path he was on and to leave behind any fear.

Frank Taylor, in turn, took to Mike Lowery, promoting him to barn foreman in his first year at Taylor Made Farm.

He was to leave the farm, however, to join Ready Made Racing at Frank's suggestion and travel to Ocala, Florida, where Will Walden, a recovering addict, and several other SR residents were working.

The work, as any person coming onto the racetrack will discover, is grueling. "We had to be there at three thirty in the morning, work till about twelve, get off work, get something to eat, and come back and feed in the evening.

"I wasn't really taking care of the spiritual side of recovery, and I was sleeping all the time when I wasn't working. I was tired. It was causing depression being eight hundred miles away.

"We came back to Keeneland, went to Churchill Downs, then went to Ellis Park.

"I got a young family. I started missing things like my son's first steps and I was like, 'Will, I gotta get back to my family. Being a father is important to me.'"

Mike was also paying rent in two places, on the road and an apartment for his family in Lexington.

Toyota has a major manufacturing plant in Georgetown, Kentucky, which is just to the west of Lexington, and Mike had lined up a well-paying job there. That is, until Frank Taylor talked him out of taking it. How did Frank do it? "It's Frank," Mike said with a long and hearty laugh. "He said, 'Look, if you come back, run one of the bigger barns for me, the next position that becomes available for management, I'll promote you.'"

Frank remembers his sales pitch to Mike: "He got a good offer from Toyota making a lot of money—more than I could pay him. I said, 'Just think about this Mike: You're going to be making five or six dollars more an hour, but is that worth it to be in a factory doing something you're probably not going to like as opposed to being out here with these horses?'"

Mike didn't need to think about it; he came to work on the farm. More than money came his way. In only a few months, a broodmare division manager retired at Taylor Made and, true to his word, Frank put him in the position. The promotion meant a home for Mike and his family on the farm without expenses for rent, utilities, or even gasoline for a farm truck to use.

"Sometimes it seems surreal, more than I deserve."

Frank Taylor would disagree. "He's a working machine. And he's got a great attitude. He's grateful and he took to it like a duck to water."

If his earlier stint at Taylor Made was impressive, his time on the racetrack confirmed that work ethic he demonstrated at DV8. "He got with Ready Made," said Frank, "and worked almost a full year and become their lead guy running their shedrow. He'd never put on a bandage starting out, but he can do anything. He could go right now and run a shedrow for anybody."

His responsibilities now at the farm are immense. To put it into perspective, the broodmare band at Taylor Made Farm is the largest in central Kentucky. In all likelihood, that also makes it the largest in the world.

At any given time, Mike's management spans 150 to 200 broodmares and their foals spread over five barns. Foremen in each barn report to Mike along with a crew of grooms, many of whom are SR residents.

Mike knows the story behind each man from SR and what is happening through both their work and recovery program. He knows, as he did with his own life, what is at stake.

"I see a father getting their son back. I see a child getting their dad back. I see a blessing from God because I know how many people die each year because of overdose." His words echo those that Frank Taylor often speaks.

He knows, also, the ways in which the School of Horsemanship is a blessing no other program can offer. "When you come to the farm, the great thing is, you don't have to look for a job. That stressor is eliminated.

"Overall it's just a great place because when guys get out of jail and rehab and those things, they don't have the transportation to work. Here you got a job. You don't have to pay for gas to get there. All you have to do is just work. You're set up."

There are other things that most everyone takes for granted, like Social Security cards and other IDs. "A lot of guys like myself, we didn't have that stuff."

There are careers, as well. "I tell guys, 'Hey, even if the horse industry isn't what you want to do, you can build your foundation and go from there.'"

Mike maintains his own foundation through sponsorship of, in his words, "a lot of guys," not surprising given a happy demeanor that would cause addicts to instinctively say to themselves, "I want what he's got."

He uses the famous Big Book of A.A. with sponsees and goes through a chapter a week with them. He also talks to his own sponsor weekly. "In the beginning, it was every day the first year."

Working your program, as those in recovery call it, is essential no matter how good life may be. "Sometimes, especially now, I can find myself getting caught up in the day-to-day, the responsibility I have now, but I'm pretty good at recognizing that and getting back to where I need to be."

Proximity to another addict throughout the workday is one more benefit to being in SR. "If you come up and say, 'Man, I'm struggling right now,' I'm going to stop and help you."

Mike's own small network of support is a lifeline for him. He struggled in trying to express what Christian Countzler has meant to him both in his early recovery days at the Shepherd's House and now at SR. "That's my guy."

When asked about Frank Taylor he laughs a laugh that comes easily to him. "That's my guy, too. I'm forever grateful, forever loyal to him because I can relate to him. You see what he's got going on, the money he's invested in it himself. He invested his own money on three drug addicts who weren't even sober a year yet.

"He doesn't expect anything else but for you to try to do right. Professionally, it's the same type of deal. He rolls in my division, and he'll nitpick the hell out of things, but I know it's to develop not only my eye but my management of people."

Lastly, he offers a surprising and odd-sounding, yet authentic, summation of a relationship with God, his Higher Power: "He's my buddy."

What Christian, Frank, the other SR residents, the horses, and his Higher Power give Mike is the most valuable thing he can have. "This has given me a purpose for my whole life. I never had a reason to get up in the morning.

"It's hard to explain the connection with the horses."

It is a connection silently made permanent through a kind eye.

15

"Are You Out?"

Honestly, truthfully, they all accepted me. . . . They knew that I was there to get sober.

—JOHN BOWMAN

To ask the question that is this chapter's title is a delicate matter. John Bowman is gay. He neither advertises that he's gay or denies it when it comes up. Students in middle school and high school called him names daily. He is simply "John" in Stable Recovery.

John is an SR "legacy," which identifies him as having a year of sobriety. He is now a peer support specialist for a Lexington recovery center. Through sobriety and recovery, he desires to help others. "If [others are] working a program—a true spiritual program—recovery absolutely trumps anything else, no matter what kind of walk of life you live, no matter who you are," John said, adding this to emphasize it: "If they're truly, deep down, entrenched in A.A. and that way of life, then they'll accept anybody for who they are."

John's personal life isn't the reason for a profile in this book. Instead, it is about sobriety after twenty-four years of addiction; recovery that has launched him into a career working with addicts . . . and an aptitude with horses that made him, as Frank Taylor calls it, a "natural horseman."

Christian pulled him out of the School of Horsemanship halfway through to work at Taylor Made on a level equal to experienced horsemen and horsewomen. He went on to Spy Coast Farm near Taylor Made, which trains performance horses for hunting, jumping, or showing. When the position of School of Horsemanship coordinator opened up back at Taylor Made Farm, he was also a natural to fill the position.

John's ability with horses comes from, in all likelihood, understanding the relationship between horses and the residents of SR as well as himself. It may also have to do with no worries about acceptance with horses. Unconsciously, it's a good guess that an additional ability to relax and be himself with horses made them respond to him . . . naturally.

"I saw it all the time," he said, referring to the instant response of horses to his moods and attitudes and those of others around him.

"You have to have a clear mind. If you're aggravated, irritated, or anything like that, don't walk into the stall with a horse. They're going to pick up on it, and they're going to test you."

He attributes the horses' intuitiveness with humans to being emotionally intelligent.

"They have good days and bad days, but they also pick up on *your* days. If you're having a sad day, they'll notice that." "Nicer" is the word John used to describe the concern a horse will show with humans who are down emotionally.

Others have to learn to adjust mood and attitude walking into a stall with a thousand-pound animal. John unconsciously, perhaps, enters every stall free of anxiety and free, period. Nobody is going to call him homophobic slurs in that stall. That freedom is more than a routine experience. He knows to seek it on his own time.

"If I have a bad day, I could just go see a horse.

"Typically, when I worked at the barns, I would try and make it into every single stall and put my arms around their necks and just love on them. They're God's creatures. There's just something beautiful about those horses that will lift your spirits.

"No matter what kind of day you're having, horses can always make it better."

A horse that drew his attention happened to be a filly, Wonder Wheel, who earned $1.5 million on the racetrack in a brief nine-race career. Two of those wins were in Grade 1 stakes races (the highest level of competition for Thoroughbreds). The horse touched him more than others for some inexplicable reason

The forty-two-year-old Frankfort, Kentucky, native had never touched a horse before entering SR. That might be a surprise but perhaps not if you know that nobody had ever touched John's heart before.

He described himself as a "mama's boy" growing up in Frankfort, shunned by his alcoholic father who favored an older sister. She was, according to John, the "golden child."

He doesn't believe family dysfunction, however, pushed him into twenty-four years of drug use. "It was growing up in a small town and not fitting in anywhere." That's putting it mildly. He described what he got from other students at school as "torture," accentuating his isolation.

John first found community with other gay people in Louisville, fifty miles or so west of Frankfort.

"I fit in. I actually felt like people wanted me around, and there was no judgment."

There was a downside, however. "I struggled with drugs all my adult life. Once I found meth, it's hard to get away from that."

Only seventeen, he would make his way from Frankfort to Louisville every weekend. His first trips were particularly memorable.

"I did probably all the major drugs within a two-weekend span, trying them all for the first time. The first weekend I did meth, cocaine, and ketamine [a drug used as an anesthetic for surgery]. The next weekend, I did acid [LSD], 'G' [GHB, a liquid version of the drug Ecstasy] and something else I can't remember."

It wasn't long before he knew he was an addict and made efforts to stop using. He tried for the wrong reason. "I was trying to get sober for my family and not really for myself—just for my mom. It never really worked out well. I always relapsed."

At age forty-one, he decided to try rehabilitation.

He had heard about Stepworks in London, Kentucky, a live-in detox and recovery center that treated men for thirty days. He fit in there, too.

"Honestly, truthfully, they all accepted me. They all knew that I was there for a reason. They knew I was there to get sober and to make my life better."

Nobody had any issues with his sexual orientation.

Integrated with nightly A.A. and N.A. (Narcotics Anonymous) meetings, he found encouragement to find a sober living home or long-term residential rehabilitation facility beyond thirty days. Other Stepworks patients warned him that he was "doomed" if he didn't take this next step.

John was adamant about *not* following this advice. He had an IT job waiting for him when he left Stepworks.

The advice was prescient; the job lasted two days.

"They knew that I had gotten a DUI and I had been arrested." His employer knew this before the job offer when John got out of Stepworks, but "legal stuff" necessitated his firing.

His attorney handling his DUI case had advised him either to get a job or go into long-term treatment. John had a "Hobson's choice"—a free choice when actually there is only one. Ironically, the term originated with a stable operator named Hobson in the nineteenth century who, to preserve his better horses from overwork, offered patrons only one lesser choice to take or leave.

John's choice was something he had heard about: Stable Recovery.

He called his therapist at Stepworks for contact information. Ten minutes later Christian Countzler called him to tell him about how intense the program was. He followed that with only a few questions.

"'Well, when can you get here? How about tomorrow? Can you stay sober till then?'" John recalled.

The next morning at 11:00 John was a new resident at SR.

"I had nothing to lose," he said. "What could it hurt? It's just a year out of my life that I could get better."

"Better" is the key word with his decision. He was determined to stay sober a full year and faithfully pursue recovery. Mission accomplished and ongoing.

An important next step was getting Christian's blessing to accept a job outside of SR. It is routine for men to ask Christian's opinion on readiness for departure from the program. With John, it was not following a routine as much as respect. "I had asked Christian before I started looking for peer support positions. I pulled him aside and I asked him for his blessing because I knew I wanted to go where they did not have peer support. Christian's response was 'Absolutely.'"

John began in the position in August 2024. As a legacy he could still live at Preston House. He chose to.

Asked his primary takeaway from his time at SR he responded, "It is to help other people.

"The only way that I can keep this and stay sober is by helping others, no matter who they are, no matter what they're doing. They always say the most important person in the room is the newcomer."

There's actually an old A.A. adage, "You can't keep what you don't give away."

John simply wanted to fit in. He did so with Christian Countzler, with the men of SR, and with horses.

16

Horses and a Higher Power

*The things horses did for me, from the very beginning,
are things that a human being never could.*

—KYLE BERRYMAN

"Horses were my Higher Power before I had a close relationship with God," said Kyle Berryman.

Addiction asks one thing of the individual ready for sobriety and recovery: submission. For many drug addicts and alcoholics, the "group"—other drug addicts and alcoholics—is the source of "experience, strength, and hope" and can be the first Higher Power.

But it can also get a little weird. As an addict, I have been in meetings where the Higher Power for one person was his Dodge truck and for another a doorknob. (I'm not making this up.) Submission, needless to say, can be to almost anything. I thought anything beyond the group or God to be completely lame before learning there is a thread that runs through the stories of every addict no matter the Higher Power or how ridiculous it is.

Addicts have never really submitted to *anything*. A truck or doorknob actually is better than nothing because it is a feeble but initial step in the right direction. It's not *what* you submit to that is important. It is the fact you finally *did* submit to something. It's a novel experience as powerful, in its own way, as the first experience with drunkenness or a drug high.

Step 2 of the Twelve Steps of Alcoholics Anonymous is *[We] came to believe that a power greater than ourselves could restore us to sanity.* Note that it says "sanity," not sobriety. No judgment here, and make of Step 2 what you will, but generally speaking, the Dodge truck and doorknob are not the usual Higher Power, or at least they aren't after sanity sets in. It's a safe bet that somewhere along the line a spiritual Higher Power replaces them.

The obstacle to sanity is, of course, the addiction, but that word is a blanket only partially covering what addiction is: literal enslavement to a substance. The addict does not submit to drugs, alcohol, sex, and gambling as much as give the keys to life and direction to an inert substance. Step 1 is *We admitted we were powerless over alcohol—that our lives had become unmanageable.*

The key word in that step is "we." Nobody is going to be able to do it alone. It is the first word in the Twelve Steps of Alcoholics Anonymous and perhaps the most inherently applicable and appropriately beautiful.

Some people believe the bondage to an addictive substance is a disease originating in one's DNA, that some of us are hardwired to react allergically to alcohol or another substance. Others think one circumstance or another creates addiction. It's the old nature versus nurture dichotomy.

At time of writing, Kyle Berryman is a forty-two-year-old assistant trainer with Ready Made Racing on the Kentucky racing circuit. He's an amazingly articulate and intelligent man whose peace with himself, sobriety, and life in racing can lead you right away on meeting him to think, *This guy should be doing something else.* To think that is to denigrate his profession and also the power of horses in his life. Kyle is *exactly* where he needs to be, and what he has learned from horses is far more important and valuable than anything he could have learned pursuing a college degree.

Verbal gems (of which I almost have to fight jealousy) come from him naturally with ease. His description of the addict's mind, at least for him, is priceless: "The disease part of my mind is the part that's selling the bullshit. The other part of my brain is buying it."

It's an eloquent way of describing the vicious cycle of addiction with no direction but down. For Kyle, OxyContin was "everything I ever wanted in life." He honestly believed that he could live a life with this drug as the end-all and be-all.

The source of Kyle's addiction would seem to be nature—a predisposition to addiction with which he was born. "I had a great family. Minimal problems, normal problems, nothing tragic. Great upbringing. Good parents. No alcoholics. Christian home. Good friends."

None of those things, however, brought him peace. "I wasn't comfortable in my own skin. No underlying issues. I just recall, even before I abused any substances, feeling that way as a young child."

The only thing he can point to that drove him to addiction was boredom with life in Mount Sterling, Kentucky, his hometown. But he also recognizes he had friends in the same environment not suffering smothering boredom.

"I can remember when I was twelve or thirteen, ordinary life just wasn't enough to cancel out boredom." He smoked marijuana and drank, but no more or less than peers.

"But when I had my first opiate, that first Lortab, I knew that it was probably going to be a problem. I liked it that much. It was really an abnormal experience."

Lortab became part of Kyle's life after he broke his ankle during a high school football game. He was seventeen.

"That's when it started . . . opiates.

"They were my solution because it would make an ordinary day extraordinary. That's all I needed was that—that social lubricant. It got to the point where I could be by myself and be fine. It was my only friend."

It's common for addicts to refer to an addictive substance or behavior as their best friend. It got them through tough times before it turned on them as it always does. The chains secured them slowly, unbeknownst to the addict. Freedom quietly and unnoticeably slipped away.

"You get to the point you become physically addicted. Even if the mental side starts to straighten out, you have the physical side of the opiates, and you can't stop or you're going to get sick."

The football injury, or more specifically the opiate to treat it, was enough to send Kyle on a systematic, semi-frantic chase for more. "There was no 'KASPER' [Kentucky All Schedule Prescription Electronic Reporting]. You could go to multiple doctors and get whatever you wanted."

KASPER eliminated doctor hopping. A doctor in Kentucky could see if there was a prescription for a drug with another doctor and deny a second one.

"Back then, you could get six different prescriptions for the same medicine and just wear it out," Kyle said.

Addicts are typically good at two things: lying and getting what they want no matter the obstacle. "A buddy of mine, his dad was a doctor, and I found his prescription pad. I learned how to do shorthand Latin and wrote a few prescriptions," an offense that got Kyle arrested.

He graduated from high school and enrolled in Western Kentucky University, about three hours south of Mount Sterling. A student graduating with a 3.75 grade point didn't even make it a full semester, flunking out within a month and a half after getting to Bowling Green.

Strangely, Kyle doesn't recall doing a lot of opiates in his short time at Western. "I had a prescription, but I maybe wasn't necessarily abusing it because I was afraid to run out." Not doing a lot meant there was some opiate use along with cocaine and marijuana.

A return home ramped it back up.

"Lortab is hydrocodone. It's powerful but not as powerful as Oxy-Contin," said Kyle. "When I did my first OxyContin, that's when it got bad." Really bad. It led him to heroin and injecting it rather than smoking or snorting it.

"You sit down, and you don't have a care in the world and it's the best feeling on earth.

"Why would you want to say no to that?" asked Kyle. He didn't.

A milder prescription drug, Xanax, was the cause of Kyle's first trip to a treatment facility.

"I was nodding out with a sandwich when I went home from work and was just completely out of it. My mom saw me and there's no way I could convince her I was just tired from the day's work.

"I woke up in a detox center, almost nineteen, and that was my first experience with trying to stop."

Before going, however, Kyle got the standard question asked by parents: "Why in the world would you need this stuff?"

"I heard it my whole life, 'You're so bright. You have so much going for you,'" Kyle said.

"Reality is, I didn't know why I was doing it either. I just knew something wasn't right, and I didn't know what it was. But I knew what made it right. That's the only thing that I knew. There's no gray area. It was all black-and-white."

The detox center put Kyle on Methadone, which he regarded as providing a "layover" rather than help.

"I got back home with never any intentions of stopping at all. Got back, did the pills, and I just kept running. I ran probably till I was twenty-three."

A drug bust and jail did, however, bring things to a halt. He got out of jail with the help of a noted spokesperson in national A.A. circles, the late Dr. Burns Brady of Louisville. Brady, a remarkable man who helped probably thousands, intervened with the detective who handled Kyle's drug bust to get him admitted to the MARR Addiction Treatment Center in Atlanta. According to Kyle, compassion wasn't the top motivator for Dr. Brady's help with MARR. It was what he saw in him, that he wasn't hopeless. Kyle was to spend nine months there.

A pattern continued, though, on his release, beginning with a return to Mount Sterling.

"I don't know why if I was subconsciously planning my next relapse.

"I had a good job in Atlanta, had several all-clean friends, and had in my mind I wanted to go back and get with my high school girlfriend. As soon as I got back and walked into Walmart and saw one old friend, it was over."

His means of discharge on his terms from MARR is "classic addict" and not uncommon among sufferers: He had learned to beat a lie detector test, specifically lying about why he wanted to go home.

Relapse was inevitable once back in Mount Sterling for a complicated reason that gives insight into the mind and thinking process of an addict.

"I had no foundation. That's been the story of my whole life. There is no solution without God, without praying, without processing, without talking to people," Kyle said.

Recovery breaks down the barriers the addict builds between themselves and others. The key is in Step 3 of the Twelve Steps of Alcoholics Anonymous: *[We] made a decision to turn our will and our lives over to the care of God as we understood him.*

Kyle is deeply spiritual but nonreligious. That may sound contradictory to many if not most people, but it encompasses and defines a Christian worldview built through a relationship with God rather than religious observance. That God is the God *as Kyle understood him.* He relates to God as a person. Conversation with God is easy for him, but so are drug slang and profanity. He believes the God of his understanding doesn't mind either. To stifle it is to dilute authentic dialogue with God, which is prayer.

The relationship Kyle had with God when he was back home was spotty at best. "Whenever I would go back out and relapse, it was about 'I gotta get this girl,' or 'I gotta get this job.'" God, for Kyle back in Mount Sterling, was an ATM or "sugar daddy" meeting every whim. Unanswered prayers and dreams would create frustration and resentment with Kyle, leading to drug use. "Then I would have to use to get over the guilt. And then use over the guilt. Then shame comes in and you gotta use because of the shame. Another vicious cycle."

It was a cycle that twenty treatment centers around Kentucky and as far away as California could not break. Again, he points to his relationship with his Higher Power, God, as the core issue. "Basically, I didn't have God. Period.

"I always thought I could do it on my own, even though in reality God was working in my life the entire time. The fact I was still alive doing the stuff I was doing was *His* doing, but I couldn't see that."

The Shepherd's House in Lexington—instrumental in the lives of so many men in the Stable Recovery (SR) program—was the twentieth treatment center but, like the prior nineteen, not the solution.

"I had a bag of dope and was using the whole time in there," Kyle said. The result of using this time, though, was not relief or the comfort that came from his old best friend.

"I got into the worst, most horrible wave of depression that I've ever gone into. Instead of looking for another bag of dope, I found myself looking for a handgun, a way out.

"I had always said I wanted to die, but it really scared me this time because I was planning it." He was at the jumping-off place, to use a term familiar to addicts.

"I had ten toes over the edge."

He googled resources in Lexington and reached someone at a sober living home. They directed him to an administrator at SR.

"He told me about Stable Recovery and about the horses, and I guess the rest is history. I was the fourth guy at SR. They'd been open a week when I came in."

Kyle knew SR worked an A.A. program, and he knew that it could work for him, but something else was the biggest selling point for him.

"The greatest thing about 'Stable' is that you have that job right when you come in. [Residents earn $10 an hour for their labor.] I didn't have anything to worry about," a major concern for a three-time felon.

"Basic needs were taken care of. I had a great sponsor and just every-thing about the program is what I needed.

"It's the structure. I couldn't lie. I couldn't fudge on my meeting sheets like I did at the other places. The community side of it—all the guys in the house—they're going to call me on it. Not Christian or Rob-ert [Osbourn]. It's the guys that I was in there with. That's the guys I didn't want to let down."

The horses were to provide, remarkably, the spiritual side he needed.

"My first time in a stall, there was this broodmare, Academic Break. She was about seventeen-two, seventeen-three hands. [A horse's height is from the ground to the top of the back where it meets the neck. A hand is four inches. Academic Break was close to eighteen hands, or six feet tall. The average Thoroughbred is five feet, three inches tall.]

"She was easily 1,400 pounds. [The average Thoroughbred weighs be-tween 1,000 and 1,100 pounds.] She'd just had her foal.

"We were in the stall and the barn foreman had showed me what to do. He said, 'All right, get at it.' And he went on to help somebody else.

"I go in there with her, and I was absolutely terrified. She's looking down and she's got her baby with her, and this idiot—me. I know now their intuition, but I was scared to death."

Kyle discovered what most everyone will discern given enough time with Thoroughbreds: "Their eyes tell you everything. You can almost look into their soul. I know it sounds kind of corny, but it's the truth.

"I feel comfortable around them."

Comfort does not, however, mean carelessness. Every horse has a distinct personality, according to Kyle, with its own personal "love language."

"I don't go recklessly in every stall. There are certain colts that strike out at you or rear up, and there are several horses that don't want to be loved on." In that sense, they are exactly like some humans.

Most remarkable about Kyle's interaction with the horses is the care and approach he has to take with each horse individually. It requires adapting his behavior and demeanor, even if it's only for the few minutes it takes to muck a stall.

"They've taught me patience as far as stopping to think, *Okay, which horse am I going in to?* They make you think: *I can't come in real fast on this one because she'll wheel and pin me against the stall.* They make me think about my surroundings . . . what I'm doing.

"It's carried over to my personal life.

"I'm processing more thoughts with people. I'm not speaking off raw emotion like I used to. I'm wondering if what I say is going to affect somebody negatively. I have to do that with horses."

The racetrack differs totally from the horse farm. There is a fast pace that racehorses and humans feel and that they react to.

"It's go-go-go. I love it. I like the pressure. I like being part of a team."

The horses respond to the daily exercise regimen and to the fitness it produces. "They get excitable in training and are a lot more playful," Kyle said.

The regimen for the horses means mental fitness for Kyle. "My whole life prior to this was flying around loose. The regimen is so detailed here that it's taught me a lot of discipline I didn't know I had."

In the hierarchy of racetrack barns, hot walkers are at the bottom and one step below grooms. In barns with many horses, there are foremen, but in a smaller stable like Ready Made, the assistant trainer might have the heaviest load of anyone.

Kyle worked only seven months hotwalking and grooming before being promoted to assistant trainer. At the time of writing, he had been in that position four months. He acknowledges that there's a lot more responsibility, and he absolutely loves it.

"I'm the first one at the barn and last one to leave," he said with a laugh, addressing the lament among other assistant trainers that they do all the work.

Reflecting on that moment with Academic Break, Kyle sees it as a clean break from an addictive past into a present he relishes and a future he looks forward to. Characteristic for this spiritual man, he, again, sees it as a divine moment: "How could I stare into an animal's eyes and see trust and comfort? That's how I know it's God."

17

Re-Up or Rehab

I would say I woke up, but I was already awake.
—ROGER SULLIVAN

A "meth head" (methamphetamine addict) would instantly understand the quote above and get the subtle humor. Meth heads stay awake for long stretches ... *really* long stretches. It's not unusual for them to stay up "for three, four, or five days, weeks, or till your body shuts down," according to Roger Sullivan.

Roger was a meth head in the past and also a dealer. "I was never a person who'd get really high and not work. I didn't take stuff apart or sit and play video games for days. I never had that issue," he said, referring to heavy users who do virtually nothing but stay high.

"I was never homeless either," he added.

A lot of the time, however, his home was courtesy of Kentucky's judicial system. That included every state prison except two, he said. In total, three stretches cost him eleven and a half years behind bars, almost one quarter of his life. He is forty-eight at the time of writing.

"I was definitely on the drug dealing end of it. I was nonstop on the go." Any drug use was between sales for Roger in his hometown of Louisville, Kentucky.

How does someone become a meth dealer? For Roger, the job dropped in his lap. Literally. A buddy dropped a pound of meth in his lap with the instruction, "'Here you go, man. Sell this. Make you some money. When you get x amount of dollars, come back, and see me.'"

Roger wasn't certain about the proposition. "I said to him, 'I never sold this before in my life.' He said, 'Don't worry about that; it sells itself.'"

Drug dealing wasn't new for Roger. He had sold OxyContin, trafficking prescriptions—"scripts"—until arrested. That earned him his first trip to prison, where he served eighteen months before being granted parole.

The pound dropped into his lap was worth $7,000 at the time. In Roger's hands, that turned into $11,000, a lucrative profit by any standard. Quick turnover of product and replenishing supplies added to his business.

"I wasn't selling grams," he said, which would have meant as many as twenty-eight separate transactions. (There are twenty-eight grams in an ounce.) "I was selling ounces at a time to people.

"Me personally, I was in it for the quick dollar. I'd rather make a couple of hundred dollars a few times a day than I would run around selling grams all day long." His business model was a good one: Fewer sales but in larger quantities and more money per sale.

The kind of money Roger was making in 2004–2005 was during methamphetamine's infancy on the streets. "People frowned upon it. You just didn't go around asking, 'You know where I can get some meth?'" That soon changed, and meth was all over the country, Roger said.

More supply and more dealers brought the cost down for a growing number of customers. The days of $7,000-a-pound meth and $4,000 profit were long behind Roger and other dealers. By 2016, he was buying a pound of meth for $2,600. Broken down into ounces costing $200, that meant $3,200 and a mere profit of $600.

Police, of course, were one hazard of the business but not the only one. He and a friend were involved in a shoot-out at a major intersection in South Louisville in broad daylight on a Saturday afternoon.

"He [his friend] got shot. Damn near killed him, I don't know how, but the bullets missed me. I guess the Big Guy was looking out for me that day."

Roger thinks as many as twenty to thirty bullets hit the car he was in.

ROGER GREW UP IN LOUISVILLE'S GERMANTOWN, A QUIET, COMPARATIVELY crime-free neighborhood midway between Bardstown Road (Louisville's Haight-Ashbury during the 1960s) to the east and the University of Louisville campus to the west.

"I had a good childhood. Both parents were in the home till they died.

"I never saw my parents fight. The only thing missing was church on Sunday." Their deaths, particularly his mom's in 2008, were a turning point in Roger's life . . . a turn in the wrong direction. "I kind of really hit the streets full speed and never really looked back."

He also split up with his first wife.

"After mom died, I just didn't really care about anything. I didn't feel like I had a purpose anymore. Nobody was there in my corner."

At a late age, thirty, Roger became addicted to meth. He firmly believes he was addicted with his first use. "It was on," he said, and added that he was a "hyper kid" probably predisposed to meth addiction. The lifestyle that came with it sank a hook deep within him. He described it as "madness" and chaotic. "I *was* the chaos."

Meth cost him his marriage and the job he was working, which propelled him into selling drugs. He also began the cycle of losing his freedom to prison sentences.

His second felony conviction was for trafficking methamphetamines and violating parole in possession of a handgun. That sentence was thirteen years. He ended up paroled after forty-two months. Charges for the third arrest and conviction were identical, except this time he was selling an unlicensed handgun. "They gave me twelve [years] and I did thirty-one months." His release was in December of 2020.

Not knowing what to do on the outside, he applied logic, or lack thereof typical for an addict. "I got out of the penitentiary, and I was sober for a couple of months. Then I came up with a great idea: I'd just sell a little bit of drugs. Before I knew it, it was full-blown, wide-open dealing again. Surprise!"

Meth and dealing had lost their allure, however. "I just got tired of it. All the BS that comes with it—in and out of the penitentiary. I thought, *I can't get in trouble no more. I ain't got that in me.* I knew there was better out there."

But it wasn't in his hometown.

"I went to bed one night and woke up with a choice I had to make. I could either re-up with some more drugs or go to rehab." He had already googled rehab facilities and saw Recovery Works in far western Kentucky in Mayfield.

"They came to my door and picked me up the same day I called them."

He was in Mayfield almost two months, doing in-patient therapy for twenty-eight days then patient hospitalization programs (PHPs) for another twenty-eight.

He'd gain sobriety in Mayfield as well as weight.

"To be honest, the first two months of it, I did a whole lot of sleeping and eating," earning him the nickname "Big Rog."

Toward the end of discharge from PHP, he learned that the authorities were going to send him back to Louisville.

It was the last place he wanted to go, knowing he would return to meth, addiction, and dealing. "After a couple of weeks, I started doing a little research on other rehab facilities. I knew I had to go somewhere else. Louisville was not going to be an option for me. I told my counselor there at Mayfield, 'I'll be homeless before I go back to Louisville.'"

Roger's counselor there succeeded in getting him sent to Recovery Works Georgetown, just north of Lexington, four hours across the state from Mayfield. Christian Countzler, among others, would make a stop there on his way to Stable Recovery (SR). His counselor's instructions were to "take it a little more seriously and look into what you can do next."

As he neared release in Georgetown, something happened that, perhaps, gives credence to what many people call divine intervention.

"They had this little waiting area at PHP at Georgetown, and I went over to a phone and made a call.

"There was a bulletin board in front of me. I just happened to look right in the middle of it and there was this little piece of paper about Stable Recovery. I hung up the phone to read it and thought, 'Huh, a job and a program.'" He asked his counselor there in Georgetown about SR. She said she knew a guy really well connected with it, and she would see what she could do. The guy just happened to be Christian Countzler. Two weeks later he had an interview with Christian, and, on release from the Georgetown PHP, he made a beeline for Hummingbird Lane in Lexington and SR.

"She was one of the people that saw I wanted to do good and be sober." She was that someone who may have been the first to be in his corner since his mother's death. "She went the extra mile for me."

Residents must spend ninety days at Hummingbird before transfer to Preston House at Taylor Made Farm. For Roger, however, he was at Hummingbird only a month and a half. "I'm good with structure. I'm good with set times. I'm cool with weekly routines."

Like most of the residents of SR, he had never touched a horse, much less worked with them. Maybe surviving gunfights and prison had prepared Roger for anything, but he was comfortable with the horses instantly. "From day one, I grabbed ahold of the thing and just started doing it. I guess the horses sense that, you know?"

Roger engages in much self-deprecating humor but said frankly and seriously about his experience in the School of Horsemanship, "I consider myself a good horseman.

"I liked the horses. They brought me a lot of peace and they humbled me."

They also impacted how he looked at recovery and its sustainment. He sees horses as a metaphor for life as an addict. "A horse can do whatever he wants at any time." For Roger, another word can easily follow the word "whatever": relapse. He could do whatever, too, but not without consequences.

"I always had my mind on the horse." Recovery, too, demands that same constant mindfulness.

Given his knack and comfort with horses, Roger went to work for Taylor Made's maintenance department after the School of Horsemanship. "I had some health problems," he said. Following that, he served as a night watchman on the farm.

Self-deprecation comes through again when Roger talks about "that whole God thing.

"I was a late bloomer on that part of the program.

"I just prayed to the sky. I put it out there and I knew something grabbed me. I've always felt like when I was out there doing drugs and stuff and doing no good, God didn't want to hear from me."

Hospitalization in Lexington for congestive heart failure and chronic obstructive pulmonary disease gave him time to test whether God would listen.

"I couldn't understand that I was sober but getting so damn sick with so many health problems.

"I had a long, long talk with him [God]. I kind of made amends. I said, 'If you're my Higher Power, show me something. Put something in front of me that's going to convince me of this.'

"God did the next morning."

While curtained off in his hospital room, a "little guy," in Roger's words, appeared mysteriously without notice. "He said, 'I'm the hospital minister.'

"The first thing I thought was, *How in the hell are you sitting there and how in the hell did you see me?*"

The little man prayed with Roger and then left. *There is your sign right there*, Roger felt. He never saw the man again. He thinks he was "maybe an angel."

Released from the hospital, Roger was able to return to Preston House. "Hospital didn't affect my spot here at Stable Recovery. I'm still here."

He has performed a variety of duties and positions for the program. He was house manager at Hummingbird a couple of times a month and was senior manager at Preston House, which means he oversaw the house manager.

Ironically, for someone who spent years driving around Louisville making drug drops, his main task at times for SR was driving residents around Lexington to court dates, probation meetings, meetings with parole officers, and doctor's appointments.

In his time at Preston House he appreciated that he could walk out the back door and find horses right there.

"They bring me peace," something not easily found for someone who struggled with hyperactivity as a child.

"Maybe it's the freedom they have. They drift around with no worries. They know that they're going to be bathed. That they're going to eat."

Horses will mirror human behavior. Outside the door of Preston House, Roger saw himself in that same mirror. He, too, is free.

18

Five Deaths Plus His Own

I died for twenty-six minutes.

—WILL JACKSON

As stated earlier, a lot of addicts like the notion or idea of sobriety and recovery but discover that continuing in addiction is preferable to the work—the Twelve Steps of Alcoholics Anonymous, accountability, rigorous honesty, vulnerability, making amends, disclosing all the dirt to loved ones, developing character, and more things than what I've already listed. In short, getting clean and sober is a whole 'nother proposition. One wag and veteran of recovery has always said that the Twelve Steps are really two steps. Step 1: stop drinking, drugging, gambling, and so forth; Step 2: change everything else about your life.

Purdue University bills its ten-foot drum in the school's marching band as the World's Largest Drum. A drummer who could somehow get a drum roll out of it is the only thing proper for introducing the sobriety and recovery rate of Stable Recovery (SR). As mentioned several times already, it bears repeating again: At the time of writing, the SR program has achieved, for a ninety-day program, a clean and sober rate as high as 94 percent over ninety days. The national rate for addicts over live-in ninety days is both paltry and tragic: 12 percent.

Will Jackson is a slightly built, soft-spoken, sandy-haired man who earned the nickname "Smiley" in high school. To this day—and Will is forty-seven at the time of writing—it is rare not to see him smiling. He is a part of that 94 percent in SR. The stories of each man in this Part 2 are deeply moving, amazing, and, to a great extent, miraculous. Will's story, however, might put him at the top in hardship, twists and turns, and survival that defy explanation.

Will was dead for twenty-six minutes yet came through that without brain damage.

That's just for starters, though. He's had the misfortune of discovering a bizarre, bewildering number of dead people; a childhood bouncing between a mother and sister in different states; an extended family of alcoholics, drug addicts, convicts, and marijuana growers; and a wife dead from cotton fever (more on this later). And that's not covering Will's immersion into drugs and alcohol and a near-death experience.

Will never met his biological father, who flew the coop before he was born. A stepdad followed who went to prison when Will was five years old, sentenced to life plus forty-nine years. (Don't ask me how, but it's possible.) He was found guilty of the murder of an elderly couple. While there were three accomplices, Will's stepdad was the only one caught, tried, and convicted.

"He served thirteen years of his sentence and died of cancer in the Arkansas State Prison.

"My mom owned a bar in Missouri. I have vague memories of that and pictures of me in cowboy boots up to my hips playing pool with Hells Angels," said Will.

Whether to allow Will to escape his stepdad before prison or her alcoholism isn't clear, but his mother sent him from Missouri to Kentucky to go to kindergarten and live with a sister fifteen years older than him.

The environment there wasn't much of an improvement, if any, to a bar and Hells Angels.

"As young as I can remember, all my aunts, uncles, and other family members either drank, smoked pot, took pills, or all three. I started out with cousins my age or close to it. Their parents did it, so we started out real young.

"One of my cousins I was close with grew pot, and I helped harvest it every year. I'd guard it, sleep beside it, take care of it, and harvest it. I was smoking and even taking pills—just a small amount—when I was probably eleven years old."

Despite the family culture or lack thereof, Will grew up with a different life in mind.

"I swore I'd never drink because of my mom. I did really good in school and I had aspirations of getting a college degree."

Will had a dream of becoming a social worker and helping people. But this dream may have gone off the rails when he was twelve years old and a sister to the one he was living with in Kentucky committed suicide.

"She shot herself in the head. I went into her house and saw all that.

"She was five years older than me." He added something suggesting trauma: "I got pretty angry."

Despite a family where "a lot of my family drank themselves to death" (and Will drank to blacking out as early as age twelve), he said he was never a "steady alcoholic" until a few years later after marrying the first time.

A year at Eastern Kentucky University came before that, and the second of a string of deaths. A friend, age sixteen, died when he slipped on the ladder of a railcar and fell between the cars.

"A year or two after that, my girlfriend, at the time, and me got into an argument. She was drinking and left drunk, ran into a tree, and it killed her.

"So much stuff kept happening with the people around me that I was close to," an understatement of mammoth proportions.

More death was to happen, including his own.

He married a stripper and, defying all odds, stayed married for thirteen years.

"She was wild as a buck, five years older than me," Will said. "She'd been married to a drug dealer and she had a gambling addiction playing Texas Hold'em poker.

"She'd lose the car in a poker game one night and then on another night she'd come home with $10,000 in cash and throw it on the bed."

Will worked a series of factory jobs and at a grocery. But it all came to a bad end because of problems in his marriage.

"The first year, the two of us were fine. After that, it was all fighting and arguing.

"I could keep a job for a year or two but then, with our fighting and her calling where I worked, I'd wind up losing good jobs."

He had smoked pot and taken pain pills and Xanax "and whatever [he] could find," while at EKU. He believes drinking didn't become a problem until much later after marriage.

That ended when his wife died from a freakish occurrence known as cotton fever caused by accidentally injecting cotton from the tip of a needle with cocaine or another substance.

"When you shoot up, you draw the drug through cotton. The cotton gets into the needle tip, gets in your vein, rots, and gets into your bloodstream," Will explained. She contracted pneumonia and died.

Will returned to his mother's house and began drinking heavily, grieving both the death of his wife and the end of his marriage.

He got a job with a home builder and drank from sunup on, even driving workers to projects in a work van when he was drunk.

"I worked for seventeen years and never missed a day drinking that heavy." He estimated he would drink a quarter of a fifth of vodka before getting behind the wheel. Somehow, he never was involved in a traffic accident.

He remarried and is blunt about his condition at the time. "My wife fell in love with a drunk, but she was quiet about it.

"On my wedding day I was drunk.

"It got bad enough that I developed spots on my legs. I found out I had fatty liver. Both liver and kidneys were shutting down and they told me I had less than a year to live. Cirrhosis was setting in. I was thirty-six or thirty-seven years old then."

Maybe because he had seen so much death and now faced it himself with his own prognosis, Will stopped drinking and began going to Alcoholics Anonymous meetings with his wife.

He conquered alcohol, but drugs were still a big part of his life.

"I got introduced to Suboxone on the street," he said, a drug supposed to curb cravings for alcohol and opioids.

A doctor prescribed it for six months that turned into five years for Will. When he did stop using Suboxone, the result was, in his words, "The worst thing I'd ever come off of, worse than any kind of withdrawal. It was horrible and it lasted a month."

Amazingly for a drug meant to help with alcoholism, Suboxone turned Will to heroin for the first time in his life.

"A little here and a little there and before you know it, I was hooked on heroin." Amazingly during this time, he found yet another dead body, this time one of his best friends, in a shed behind his home. Will felt as if this discovery somehow signaled things coming to a head in his life.

"I had not done heroin for some time, but I was taking Xanax and telling myself I was getting off heroin when I was really doing something stronger.

"One night I was taking a bunch of Xanax and ran into my connection for heroin. Of course, he gave me a tiny bit." He waited until he was home before using.

"My wife was asleep. It was two in the morning and I had some pot on a plate. I decided I would do that little bit of heroin and I fell to the floor and died. I OD'd. The only thing that saved me was the plate breaking when I dropped it. It woke up my wife."

EMTs came to Will's home and administered "two or three four-milligram doses of Narcan." That is not a small amount.

Will's answer to what to do next was right out of the addicts' handbook on how to be stupid: He kept using but "cutting back."

About to lose his job, he went to his boss and confessed, telling him he needed help.

"When he heard the word 'heroin' it was all over," said Will. He fired Will on the spot.

Will went to a hospital and in his words "begged for help." They sent him to Stepworks, which has facilities all across Kentucky offering a full spectrum of recovery programs. Irony of ironies, Will went to Stepworks in Nicholasville, Kentucky, the home of both Taylor Made Farm and Preston House, SR's largest home for residents.

"My counselor there had a one-page flyer on Stable Recovery. Nobody had ever heard of it; nobody had ever been to it from there; nobody knew anything about it. All I knew was one of the residences was on a farm.

"I'd been on a farm once when I was young and I always dreamed of being back on one.

"I could drive a tractor before I could say my ABCs," he added with a laugh.

"It was all a miracle that it came around the way it did.

"When I ended up at Stable Recovery, I had botched everything up. We were in a house sixteen years. I lost it. I lost my truck. I got us evicted. I left my brother for the house building job I got fired from. That was hard on him."

Although sober, he was not safe at home just yet. He stayed first at the Hummingbird Lane house in downtown Lexington before moving out to Preston House.

"SR had not been operating very long—four or five months. It was really early in the stages of it and there'd been a couple of groups of guys. There wasn't hardly anybody out at Preston and nobody had been through a year."

Things weren't solidified yet either. The Kentucky Career Center, which had funded the program, stopped their financial underwriting. There was no pay for the residents.

Will moved in anyway, volunteering to work for no pay . . . for fifty-seven days with no days off.

He bypassed the School of Horsemanship that would have meant pay for SR residents. "As a volunteer I could go anywhere on the farm where I was needed. I went straight into a barn, a foaling barn, Bonaterra C, getting training from the other workers as well as the barn foreman.

"The foreman had been here eighteen years. By the time everything got straightened out with funding and they were ready for me in the School of Horsemanship, I'd already been there long enough that the manager didn't want me leaving the barn. I was trained in horsemanship already," he said with a laugh.

Will also kept volunteering on his days off even after getting paid.

"Christian uses it as an example all the time because the guys get to whining about money after a week or something. He'll say, 'Will came in here and worked fifty-seven days straight, didn't ask for money, and didn't complain.'"

He was the first SR resident to transition from Taylor Made.

The farm has a ninety-day probationary period before someone can go on the Taylor Made payroll. Managers then meet to evaluate prospective employees.

"I was the first guy through our program voted unanimously by all the managers. I was really proud of that," he said with a smile bigger than the usual one gracing his face.

Like all novice farm and SR workers, it was initially intimidating to get next to a 1,200 to 1,500-pound Thoroughbred mare.

"At first, some of them want to fight with you. They'll pick on you when they know you're afraid, and you don't know what to do. They'll put their hoof down and move on you and just do all kinds of stuff to aggravate you because they know you don't know what you're doing."

It's a process that involves time for both horse and human.

"The more comfortable you get with them, the more comfortable they are with you," he said.

"After a little while of doing, you learn to be gentler with them. As much as you think you're in control, you can't really make them do anything. You ask them to do things. They want to do things to make you happy; they really do.

"You learn everything takes a little finesse. You gotta move with them and not jerk and grab and push. You learn to just give them little gestures. They already know what to do and they know if they want to do it. If they want to buck, they'll tell you. Once you start getting comfortable and can keep your heart rate down, they start doing everything you want them to do. They'll pick their feet up and stand there for you. But it takes you getting a bond going with them.

"You have to let go and give in to the power of the horse. You have to give in and know that you have no power to do anything. It becomes a relationship.

"You have to submit completely."

Submission to the power of a horse parallels recognition of powerlessness and the unmanageability of alcohol or drugs. The horse both represents and points to a Higher Power.

"The relationship you build with the horse does it. You don't even know it's happening.

"When I could finally let go and see everything happening with the horse, somehow it allowed me to relate the situation to a Higher Power and the whole program.

"The way you link up with the horse, you can't be somewhere else. Your mind can't be thinking about how you didn't make your bed. It can't be what you're going to say to your wife when you talk to her. You learn to actually focus on the moment and be here now . . . be in that moment. You can't be anywhere else.

"As you learn and get more comfortable with it, it's because you fall in love with the horse, and it'll be that way with people too.

"When I could finally open up and see the physical part of it with the horse, it opened me up to seeing the spiritual part with my life.

"You also get this 'aha' moment when you believe you can go on with your sobriety."

Will, at the time of writing, is a facilities manager for SR but is actively involved with the residents, as are all executive staff and other associates of the program. He passes on his "experience, strength and hope," as the Big Book of A.A. expresses it.

That dream of helping people has come true.

19

Suspended. Surviving. Sober.

Shyness is invariably a suppression of something. It's almost a fear of what you're capable of.
—RHYS OWAIN EVANS

Blane Servis has a theory on why horses change a human's heart to synchronize with theirs, and it is an interesting one.

"They always sync heartbeats with one another in herds so that if some kind of predator is approaching and one notices it and starts acting a little crazy, it sends shockwaves through the whole herd. They can then get the hell away from the situation." (Interestingly, in the Afterword to this book, Dr. Ann Baldwin, physiology professor emerita at the University of Arizona, verifies Blane's theory from research.)

As noted in Chapter 10, synchronization won't occur if a human is sending negative signals—body language that indicates fear and apprehension. Could it be that someone approaching a horse with positivity indicates safety to some degree, like another herd member? Does that trigger protectiveness within the horse of that human?

Blane's background, for what it's worth, gives much credence to any and all observations he might make on horses. He is the son of Thoroughbred trainer John Servis, trainer of 2004 Kentucky Derby winner Smarty Jones and perennial placeholder in the top 100 trainer rankings in earnings every year since 2000.

Blane also trained from 2013 to 2021, his horses winning at a respectable 14 percent. He spent childhood and adolescence at the track and is, without question, the most experienced horseman among the Stable Recovery (SR) community currently.

It's almost automatic to assume that Blane's alcoholism stemmed from a racetrack environment rife with drinking. Nope. Nor was there trauma or bad relationships within his family. Given how he fell into alcoholism, it is easy to surmise that he preferred horses to humans.

Blane cannot pinpoint a reason. He simply experienced anxiety and was generally shy around people for as long as he can remember. Alcohol became the stress reliever for discomfort in social situations. "When I drank a certain amount, I had no fear to be able to act the way that I felt like I should."

It was what he felt people wanted to see. "I wasn't able to actually deal with the way I was feeling about myself.

"Being shy and anxious around people, before you start drinking, you don't really notice it. But then once you drink and all that goes away—all those fears—that's when you get hooked. You think at that time that's the answer."

His parents were supportive but baffled by this issue with their son. "They tried to do the best that they could. It wasn't their fault at all."

Schooling at Valley Forge Military Academy for high school didn't solve the problem but taught Blane a principle he would later encounter again at SR.

Students at the military academy enroll and enter the school in groups and remain with that group through the school's bootcamp. "If one person is messing up, the whole team is paying for it, which makes everyone hold each other accountable. In turn, because of the stress and the work that you're putting in and the effort that it takes to get through this period of time, it brings you all so much closer together."

SR mirrors this, said Blane. "We all come in here broken. Everybody is pushed to the limits when they first come in here, doing all these things that are changing their life. It's all happening at the same level with all of us, and you just naturally build a brotherhood."

Like every addict, Blane experienced a bottom that was more than just one event but a life that became a matter of surviving day to day.

Consequences of this issue began with an injury to a horse he was training at Parx Racing northeast of Philadelphia, Blane's hometown. A freak injury shattered a bone when the horse he trained stepped in a hole on the track. Blane disappeared from the racetrack in the aftermath.

"At the time I had two horses, and then I just had one of my good friends overdose. It was just a bad time. I was calling somebody that I knew to take care of things, and I wasn't coming in." The individual he paid to come in and take care of the horses didn't do so properly. "The racetrack found out."

The injury and then discovery of the substitute training (or no training) of Blane's lone horse led to a suspension from Parx.

The magnitude of the effect on him is inestimable. The racetrack was somewhere he had grown up, where he had spent most of his life. It was his home.

"I kind of went through a year of just trying to regroup and figure out what I was doing and going through short spurts of white-knuckling it through sobriety for months here and there and then going on benders."

Making the suspension worse, Blane isolated himself from everybody, including family.

Glenn Brock, a vice president of Brook Ledge, a horse transport company, who has known Blane all his life, helped him get a job on a farm near Penn National, a racetrack northeast of Harrisburg, 110 miles west of Parx.

Brock had read an article about Will Walden, who had become clean and sober after eighteen different rehabilitation programs.

Brock called to talk to Blane about Will's success and asked if he would be interested in talking to him. The Servis and Walden families had known each other for years, and Blane talked to Will several times.

Will's father, Elliott Walden, a highly successful trainer with a Belmont Stakes win on his résumé and president/CEO of racing operations for WinStar Farm in Kentucky, offered him a job but with a condition.

"His stipulation was, you can come down here and there'll be a place for you to stay on the farm," said Blane. "You'll be a foreman, but you can't drink."

At the time, Blane said he was in denial about a drinking problem.

The job lasted three months. "I'm living in a room on the farm by myself, so it didn't take long for me to start drinking."

When Blane missed a day of work, Will, along with his best friend, Christian Countzler, paid him a visit to come join the SR program. "I was still kind of in denial then. I stayed with some girl that I'd met a couple of weeks previously, which ended up with me staying with her for six months."

He remembered the invite to SR, though, and made the decision to enter the program in January 2023.

In June of that year he traveled to Philadelphia to see his children for two weeks. Countzler advised that the trip was too long for him to go.

The advice was prophetic: Blane relapsed after flying back to Kentucky.

"I didn't reach out," he simply said. "I was supposed to go back into the program, and I made a stupid decision to stay with that girl again."

Perhaps his first foray into recovery in SR laid groundwork that wasn't immediately apparent. "It was the first time I ever actually tried to work steps and had the willingness to actually listen and do anything asked of me."

Only an addict can know the unconscious insanity of, as the Bible states, returning to your own vomit: "Like a dog that returns to his vomit is a fool who repeats his folly" (Prov. 26:11). Blane relapsed yet again.

"I was kind of taking things for granted. What the relapse did more than anything when I came back was really humble me."

Step 1 of the Twelve Steps of Alcoholic Anonymous states, *We admitted we were powerless over alcohol—that our lives had become unmanageable.* Some in Alcoholics Anonymous say this is the only step an alcoholic can do perfectly. That's because there is no hedging or gray area in admitting powerlessness. You either own up to it or you don't, humbled by powerlessness or fooling yourself.

Like many alcoholics and addicts, Blane responds only to structure. There has to be daily submission to maintain and sustain sobriety and walk in recovery.

"You can get comfortable and kind of stop working at it. You can't do that at Stable Recovery because there's the accountability with each other that isn't at other places. The amount of effort and work you have to put in daily is something that just naturally creates brotherhood, which is unlike any other place, any other rehab you can go to." As well, program and management staff at Taylor Made Farm review and evaluate every single SR resident in the program weekly based on daily performance.

"Daily" is the operative word for an addict seeking sobriety and recovery. "Say you're slacking in something just a little bit for two weeks in a row, they're gonna call you and talk to you. And they're gonna expect to see a change," said Blane.

"At other rehabs, stuff will just get overlooked and the guy will just keep going slowly down and bounce when they leave . . . relapse. There's not as much attention to the guys as there is here.

"Stable Recovery requires you to do the steps, have a sponsor within a week [of entering the program], and meet with them every week," Blane said.

"I've learned with my relationship with God, I can truly say today that I'm actually living life. Stable Recovery helped get me in the right direction to build this relationship. It has made me a completely different person today."

Blane has also discovered a new relationship with the horses much different from anything on the racetrack and his life there.

A horse farm is a wholly distinct and different world from the racetrack. The track, of course, is the destination for horses from the farm, the finished product of a lot of hard work. The tasks of trainers there are working out horses daily, selecting races for them, and getting them to the starting gate. On the farm, there's much more: breeding, foaling (birthing babies), weaning, training yearlings, and preparing them for sales. Racehorses are in barns for a couple of years, ideally, but the routine is the same. On horse farms like Taylor Made, things change often as a colt or filly matures.

Blane, like every other person who enters SR, went through the School of Horsemanship.

"I came in during foaling season. It was my first experience being able to witness a foal being born live in front of me. And then I ended up foaling out last year probably fifteen or twenty horses.

"It gave me a deeper appreciation, being able to see the very beginnings and the work that goes in to get them to the point I'm seeing at the racetrack.

"Then I started working with the yearlings and I did yearling prep for a couple of months. Being able to see the whole progression up to where they will be on the track itself was pretty amazing."

Blane was able to see the development of men with the horses as well. "Some of them are afraid. But they start, they're taught, and they learn patience. They learn to respect the horses, and the horses respect them back.

"Once these guys can get over that initial fear, they learn about their life too.

"It's a lot harder sometimes, to deal with people, but I think early on in sobriety it is instrumental with a lot of these guys to face and overcome fears and become one with a horse.

"We come in broken and the horses don't care what you've done in your past or anything that you've been through. They just are there and they're going to be them. They're going to treat you the way you treat them.

"When you get to a certain point where you can get comfortable enough, you can take a huge animal and be able to do whatever you want with them. If you have one act up, you can respond correctly.

"To be able to calm that horse down and control it and do what you want to do, that is amazing, a powerful feeling."

He described the progression in personal growth for residents and the evolution of relationships with a horse: "You create this bond with the horse, and you want the horse to continue to thrive and to do the best that they can do.

"You get to a certain point that you realize you're a big contributing factor in this. The patience you have with that horse every day—the time that you take to maybe brush them off or curry them [comb their coat], the time that you take to maybe clean off legs, pick their feet, and pay close attention to the way they walk—are some of the things that are part of this," he said.

"You really start to feel your horses so well that if they're not acting right a certain day, you can pick up on it right away."

Blane sees parallels between successfully caring for and relating to a horse and relationships with others in recovery. "We're around each other so much that when guys are struggling with something or something's going on, we can tell right away before they say anything. You go to the guy because you're around them every day and ask, 'What's going on?' You know if there is something, someone is not being themselves.

"That's the same attention to detail that really makes a difference with a horse. Because they can't talk to you, the little details are so important. Those little things can give away something that could have just started with a horse. If you catch it early, you're preventing something bigger from coming.

"It's the same with recovery, if you can catch the little things early enough, you can use the tools you've learned to stop it from progressing too far and to redirect it."

Not surprisingly, Blane is probably the best example for other SR residents struggling with horse care because of the ones he's drawn to.

"I tend to fall in love with the horses that I wouldn't say are mean, but more of a handful.

"It's more of an effort that you have to put in to get them to really listen to you and do what you want them to do. It also gives you that little bit of excitement.

"And it kind of reminds me of myself sometimes."

He laughed at the inevitable bites anyone around a horse is likely to get, but this, too, may reveal personal growth and recovery.

"I know 95 percent of the time it's my fault. I've put myself in a bad situation or wasn't watching."

His response is always, "Okay, that hurt. You got me today. I'll pay more attention tomorrow."

"Tomorrows" for Blane include things he never could have imagined. "I'm at Godolphin [a major global entity in the Thoroughbred industry]. They have a barn here so I'm back on the racetrack. My suspension ended in June [of 2024]."

Those aren't the only changes in his life: The anxious, painfully shy young horseman, comfortable only when drinking in past days, spoke to four hundred persons attending SR's annual fundraising gala.

What else is Blane capable of? The world is about to see.

20

A Perfect Storm and Survival

The horses love me for me.

—ROBERT YOUNG

We see the homeless every day and subconsciously many of us probably blame them for their condition. After all, how could one fall so far as to live on the streets and in shelters? They had to have made bad decisions.

I've heard it said many, many times, hurting people hurt people. In the case of homeless people like Robert Young, homeless people hurt themselves.

A perfect storm of parental neglect, dire poverty as a child, a physical malady that went undiagnosed and then was horribly treated, and then the death of someone he was close to combined to make him depressed, suicidal, and drug addicted. His world was bouncing from one rehabilitation center to another, never finding what he wanted and needed.

Like many of us, his childhood was dysfunctional, but Robert's was far past extreme. "There was hardly ever anything to eat," he said, attributable to an alcoholic father and a drug-addicted mother. Eventually, the state removed Robert from his parents' home and put him into foster care.

The damage from malnutrition under his natural parents' roof was to both his physical and mental health initially. "I got married right after high school and eating caught up with me.

"I wouldn't eat all day, then when I got home, I would eat like a horse." He believes with certainty that food was a co-addiction to drugs in his life. Robert, who is thirty-eight at the time of writing, carried 260 pounds as an adult.

"I was diagnosed with type 2 diabetes. My gallbladder was malfunctioning, and I kept having a lot of problems in my right side—my stomach and liver area. I experienced pain with that for almost a year."

That pain drove him to "ER after ER. They would do CAT scans trying to figure out something." Doctors also "pumped me full of pain medicine," he said, which laid the groundwork for dependence on pain meds and addiction.

A year went by before he was in the hospital for a week, undergoing test after test. A specialist added another diagnosis to diabetes: "A gastroenterologist came in and told me that I had a disease called gastroparesis. It's where the muscles in your stomach don't digest food right."

The time in the hospital was the start of his addiction.

The bottom that all addicts experience—the time when Robert realized he was a drug addict needing help—came when his girlfriend overdosed and died in his presence using fentanyl. Robert estimates he also overdosed twelve times with this powerful drug. "The EMTs would arrive, give me Narcan, and I'd do it all over again."

His girlfriend's death drove him to treatment in a thirty-day program at a rehabilitation center in central Kentucky. Suicidal thoughts, however, were ahead of drug addiction as the main reason for seeking rehab. "I was afraid that if I stayed out that I was going to take my own life."

It wasn't the first time he would consider suicide.

Thirty days turned into four months during which he was clean. It did not end well, however.

"I had a job and ended up losing it from calling in from depression.

"I was still going through it with everything from my girlfriend dying, and I wasn't seeking mental health or any kind of counseling.

"I ended up getting high at a sober-living home and I went back out to the streets and lived with a cousin, and it was off to the races.

"I was staying with him doing meth and all kinds of stuff." Time with his cousin also included theft of his car and other possessions, and unpaid loans.

"I left there because I was afraid, and I went to my aunt's house who was also an addict, and she pretty much slammed the door in my face. I took off walking.

"I came to the point where I knew I had to try to get clean and do it right. I just had to. I had no other options. I never was man enough to take my own life."

A thirty-five-day stint followed at yet another rehab center.

Addiction and thought processes connected to it are baffling to a non-addict. Robert knew he had to get clean but said he "wasn't really ready yet to work a program." "Program" is, of course, part of addiction lexicon that refers to active work in learning and practicing the Twelve Steps of Alcoholics Anonymous and other rehabilitation exercises. Robert told his case manager that he wanted to return to a sober living home, preferably in Lexington.

The only place with a bed open at the time happened to be at the Shepherd's House—lived in as an addict and later managed by Christian Countzler.

"I had trouble—struggling to keep a job, or work a job, making it to and from work. It's hard when you gotta be at work at six in the morning to get up at four and walk to work.

"They were getting ready to kick me out."

His sponsor at the Shepherd's House did get the boot and ended up in the Stable Recovery (SR) program. This individual knew Christian from the Shepherd's House and passed on his phone number to Robert.

"I called him from the jump."

Like all SR residents at the time, he first went to the house on Hummingbird Lane. He remembers like a birthday his first day at Hummingbird: "October 2nd was the day in 2023."

Robert had worked with Quarter Horses at a small farm owned by his mother-in-law when he was married. In no way, however, did familiarity with this breed prepare him for Thoroughbreds.

"The Quarter Horses are gigantic babies. They'll let you do anything you want. Thoroughbreds are wild-spirited."

His experience in the School of Horsemanship on Taylor Made Farm taught him how Thoroughbreds, even the difficult ones, can change.

"Working with a horse on a daily basis, it is calming both of us down. You're in a stall and you're getting on the same page."

Robert said what virtually all SR residents say about the horses. "They react the same way that you're feeling."

He made a striking comparison of the benefits of a horse versus a therapist. "I don't always know what's going on inside of me. I can step into a stall, though, and that horse knows what's going on without me saying a word.

"I think—especially in the beginning—that caused me to dig down deeper in my own mind and in my own heart to figure out what I was going through to address it and to work through it. I started reaching out and talking to people. Most of all, I started trusting people again."

Another lesson was immediate. "I don't think I ever realized how special a horse was until I actually started working with them." He added that after time with the horses he was "coming back around to being a better person.

"I came in here not knowing anything. I didn't know how to live. I didn't know how to work a job, pay bills, or anything because of my time in addiction. I mean all that went out the window and it was like I lost it. I couldn't figure it out again. I didn't know how to love properly. I didn't know how to treat another human being."

Robert said instantly he felt the love from the horses in return for what he and the other men of SR gave them "no matter what we have done. They treated me like I still deserved to be loved.

"They love me for me," he said. It was a feeling more than an acknowledgment, and he equated it to "God feeling me.

"When you're ripping and running and doing drugs, you can't really feel much of anything. Before I came here, I felt dead inside. You don't feel like God is there." Drugs replaced and numbed feelings. Working with horses at SR brought him a reality that he embraced. "I was learning to live absent of drugs. It was just like a powerful love fell that only God can give you."

The horses also gave him "a sense of responsibility. I have failed most of my responsibilities after doing drugs. It kind of gives you back that feeling of being a man.

"I learned to be calmer. The horses taught me how to be more patient because you have to learn the horses with time because, of course, they can't talk to you. They taught me how to have more patience with things today."

Success with a horse—having that horse do what you want them to do—"gives a man confidence," he said. "It takes persistence not to give up and not to quit, not only with a horse, but anything that you're going through in your life. I used to quit everything.

"I'm not like that anymore. I put forth the effort and if, the first time, it doesn't work, I'll go back to the drawing board. I'll pray about it. I'll talk to God about it, and I'll keep trying to find ways to get what I want out of life and to do the right thing. I didn't use to do that."

Robert is forthright in expressing how he believes SR is superior to other programs. "I've come from people not giving a damn whether I succeeded in sobriety or not. That kind of hindered me searching for help because I felt like nobody gave a damn about whether I was sober or not. It was a money gimmick; it was a business.

"It was different when I got to Stable Recovery. I was surrounded by people that actually cared if I made it to my pillow being sober and waking up sober the next day.

"When you first get here, you're watching some guys. It's going to go from not trusting one another or not trusting anybody to getting to the point where you start to open up and trust your brother. You get that relationship built and you start trusting people more, and it brings you closer together. You know the guy that you're working with in that barn is just like you.

"You can fight a war with these guys."

The future for Robert is off to a surprisingly fast start. He is house manager at a potential SR location, which could become another entry portal for the program along with the Hummingbird Lane home.

"I've always lived in the past, reliving my childhood. *Why was my mom the way she was? Why was my dad the way he was? Why couldn't I have been raised as a normal kid?*

"All my 'whys' kept me in the past a whole lot. Working in a barn at Taylor Made put me in the present moment, now and today."

The tomorrows are about goals with Robert: "To get to where I want to be in life, to be a better father in my kids' lives doing the things that I need to do instead of reliving the cycle. Breaking that cycle is what I always wanted to do so my kids don't have to go through the things that I went through or become what I became through drugs."

He faced a tough decision to approach Christian about making a career move to better support his children. It brought him to tears.

"I talked to him and I was kind of choked up. Things ain't about money today, but I got three kids I want to do more for."

Robert is a former correctional officer and enjoyed that work. He has his eye on either the Blackburn Correctional Complex outside Lexington or the Fayette County Detention Center as prospective employers.

"I figured I was gonna disappoint him by talking to him about it—go down that path—but I respect Christian so damn much."

Christian doesn't employ algorithms or chisel in stone mandatory days or months in SR to decide whether someone is ready to leave the program. If a man is ready, Christian will tell him so and encourage him to pursue what he desires. The ultimate goal after sobriety and recovery is reentry into society.

"The horse has taught me how to know to surrender everything to God, and let God lead the show," said Robert.

"This place saved my life."

21

Kisses and Connections

The horses know a kiss is coming.

—JOHN DAUGHERTY

John Daugherty, to be certain, gives back to horses, as all the men do with the care required of Stable Recovery (SR) residents—grooming, feeding, walking, and so forth—and he does it with excellence. His expressions of that love beyond the caretaking, however, are describable in a word rarely if ever used in horse-human relationships involving Thoroughbreds: it is adorable. He is famous for kissing horses.

"They tell me, 'You can't do that,'" he said with a laugh that is frequent in his conversation.

How it began was innocent and touching. At the close of his workday at WinStar Farm, where he grooms horses at the farm's training center, he began a practice kind of like a happy husband and wife. "When I was getting ready to leave work and wasn't going to be with them until the next day, I'd lean over and kiss them on the side of their head and tell them to have a good night."

He would miss the horses in the time between leaving work and returning the next morning, and they probably missed him as well.

At the time of writing, John grooms six horses. Apparently horses, like humans, have their own love language.

"Every horse will just stick their head right in a feed tub as soon as you walk in with it and never take it out until done," he said. Three of the six in John's care "get 'em a bite, and then they turn toward me so I can kiss them on their cheek. Then they go back to eating. They know that kiss is coming."

If you think John's affection extends only to the "easy" horses, think again. "Josh Franks [then director of the School of Horsemanship] would laugh at me; I wouldn't take lunch with any of the other guys. I'd go take it with a horse in the paddock that was mean."

"Ricky" was that horse, a "teaser" used to test a mare's readiness to breed. (Maybe his grumpiness came from not being the stallion who would get the honors if the mare showed interest.)

It began when John was with the foals at Taylor Made in the School of Horsemanship. "I had a connection with them. I wanted Ricky to feel that connection too.

"I'd bring him some feed and go out there, sit down, and eat my lunch." It took a while for Ricky to accept feed from John, who resolved that he'd eat near that horse every day until he could pet him.

"Finally, he came over and started eating what I'd brought for him. From there, he would eat food out of my hands. Then he'd let me rub him. It got to where I could get in there with him and he'd walk up to me.

"Frank Taylor said I was the only person on the farm that could catch him," he said with a laugh.

Ricky wasn't John's first lunch companion. He had a whole herd of them with some of the foals under his care at the farm.

It is likely the connection John made with Ricky was more about him than the horse. The opposite of addiction is not sobriety but connection. It is connection that leads to sobriety and recovery.

"I guess I felt I wasn't cared about, just neglected," said John of his upbringing in Owensboro, a town of sixty thousand on the Ohio River in western Kentucky. John's parents, who had adopted him, were too busy fighting and worrying about themselves and moving toward divorce.

"I guess they were in bad places themselves. I can see that now, but right then, I just pretty much thought nobody really gives a shit."

His biological father died of a drug overdose when John was a month old and his mother, an alcoholic, put him up for adoption.

An uncle and aunt adopted him. He didn't know until he was twelve that a woman in his family was his biological mother. "I knew who she was. I knew her for a long time."

This discovery coincided with his aunt and uncle finally divorcing, also when John was twelve. It left him with a house all to himself pretty much. "I didn't like leaving the house. I was really isolated," he said.

One venture outside his home when he was fifteen resulted in trying both methamphetamine and marijuana on the same day. Of the two, the meth sank a hook deep into John.

"It was a game changer for me. It took me somewhere to a peace I'd never had. It got me friends, girlfriends, and money.

"I started dealing. By the time I was sixteen, I was selling it all the time. It was pretty crazy because I was one of the younger ones who could get it."

It also got him his first arrest when he was in a wreck with methamphetamines in the car. At the time, he was married to a girl he met when he was sixteen. A week after the birth of his first child, a son, John had a car wreck that led to arrest.

"I went to jail for twelve days for DUI and possession of methamphetamines.

"When I got out, I came home, and my family was at her mom's. I kind of felt abandoned."

His wife had known he was selling drugs but did not know the extent of it. "She kind of overlooked it," he said, adding that he had routinely passed on to her "a lot of money."

He pursued a new lawful career, going to a barber college and getting a license. He quit using meth when he started going to barber school but was drinking heavily.

"When I became a barber, I was able just to drink. I knew I had a problem, but the fact was, I never did drink at work," he said. "I knew I was an alcoholic. I'd lost my small family. It was a mess."

While he was able to quit drinking, he added other substances.

"I was wanting to change the way I felt. It wasn't anything to do with the actual drug that I was addicted to. I just needed to change how I felt about myself."

A prescription and a return to alcohol worked to do that for a time. "I was eating Xanax pills and I would drink at night. I'd get obliterated, and I ended up catching another charge for first-degree wanton endangerment for holding a gun to someone's head while I was drunk."

After release, he went to the Boulware Mission in Owensboro, which provides shelter services and a long-term self-sufficiency program for displaced men.

"That's when I started rehabs."

After Boulware, he succeeded in getting his old job back at the barbershop. "I actually went back to cutting hair and did well for a couple of years."

He was, however, using drugs the whole time.

John ended up meeting another girl. "When I met her, it was pretty crazy. I started selling a lot of meth and using a lot of it. That's all we did.

"I ended up quitting my job barbering so I could just be with her all the time. We went on for a year or so, and then we started breaking into places. When I did that, I ended up catching a whole lot of charges, which later sent me to prison. I ended up with, like, sixteen felonies, but the main one was I got caught with hand grenades."

How and why John had hand grenades escapes explanation. "My life was crazy, man. I just knew people that had them and I just had them for fun.

"I was throwing them every once in a while, with maybe somebody else around."

When the police discovered them in the trunk of John's car, they also found items from someone's home. "I took a first-degree burglary charge." That, and the grenades, which counted as a federal crime, sent John to prison at the Roederer Correctional Complex in LaGrange, Kentucky, outside Louisville.

Cutting the hair of fellow inmates got him through prison comfortably. He also filled time with "finding out who God was.

"I would go to the library, and I started checking out every book on spirituality—Buddhism, Islam, Christianity—I checked into all of them.

"I actually played guitar some in the chapel band.

"That chapel was used for Buddhists, Muslims, everything, so I got to meet a lot of guys and have deep conversations with them. I came out a Christian, even though I was trying to disprove it."

Strangely, a relationship with an alcoholic and drug-addicted girlfriend may have paved the way for John's decision.

"The girl I was with had me praying every night before dinner. We'd sit down with the kids and hold hands and pray.

"I got used to praying and kept doing it."

"Happily ever after" wasn't in the cards, however. The court granted custody of him to her in her home after two years in Roederer and a brief stay in a halfway house in Louisville.

"She was a real bad alcoholic. So, of course, I was drinking with her and I ended up getting a parole officer who didn't really care," John said.

He eventually left her and moved in with his adopted mother before going off to a rehab center back in LaGrange.

It tells a sad tale on the state of things in many rehab centers that John started using meth again while there. After moving to another rehab center in Owensboro he also started drinking again. A last stop before SR was yet another rehab facility in Hopkinsville, Kentucky.

His stay there was only twenty-eight days and it was providential for John.

"There was a lady that worked for the Goodwill in Hopkinsville. She used to work with Christian [Countzler] at Shepherd's House. She heard me talking and told me about Stable Recovery. She ended up calling him for me."

John, now a deeply spiritual man despite relapses, prayed about SR before contacting Christian. "I felt like God was telling me to go. He was. It was the best decision I ever made in my life.

"I got there on June 28th of 2023."

He immediately came into contact with Josh Franks (profiled in Chapter 11), a fellow Christian who became a close friend and confidant.

"[When] I got there, the babies, the foals, were probably two and three months old and some four. I got to do a lot of working with the mamas and the foals there. I fell in love with them."

The relationship took him into paddocks with the foals for lunch, mentioned earlier. "Josh used to make fun of me," John said with a laugh.

"He loved that I did it. He just saw how much I cared about the horses. He knew that fire he had that I also had.

"My heart was open to them. And I allowed them in.

"Those horses rely on you, they really do." John echoed what several others have said about them: "They don't judge you. They don't care who you are. They didn't care that I was out of prison and kept getting in trouble and lost everything. They wanted to know how I was going to treat them and that was amazing to me. That was a special feeling."

After he graduated from the ninety-day School of Horsemanship, WinStar Farm hired John as a groom. It required a van ride from Preston House on Taylor Made Farm to his new job before moving into a new home for SR residents at WinStar.

He said he does everything with the horses "except ride them."

His schedule is thirteen days on with one day off. John likely would be willing to work every day.

"They give me something to look forward to. I wake up happy to go to them. I can't imagine having to get up at three in the morning to go to another job."

His take on SR is a novel one: he describes it as a "reentry program."

"They get you back into society and they want you to succeed. They stay with you until you are ready to go out. The other rehabs, you gotta do the program and then you go to a sober living home that doesn't care what you do. Stable Recovery actually cares."

His introspection extends to taking apart the dynamics of the horse-human relationship and its impact on him. "I learned how to love again. I learned to love these horses first.

"They taught me that there's action behind it, the things I did for them. When I loved them, I started taking pride in it and that allowed me to care about myself.

"I started caring about what I did the night before. I didn't want to get in trouble because I wanted to make sure I was there the next day. The horses opened me up to start loving myself again.

"There's no way that God didn't give me these horses."

To love and to, yes, kiss.

22

The End of "Everlasting"

I had to learn how to be okay with Josh.

—JOSH BRYAN

On Tuesday, April 22nd, 2025, Josh Bryan died from complications following surgery in a Lexington hospital.

I can hardly imagine how hard it hit Frank and Kim Taylor and the people of Stable Recovery (SR). Josh was Frank's best friend and a son to him. It seemed like wherever you saw Frank, you also saw Josh. For the men of SR, he was the first "best friend" many of them ever had. His name came up often in interviewing the eleven other men profiled herein, and this was while Josh was living. If his death had an impact on others, his life surpassed it.

The profile below was written before his death. It was adapted only slightly after April 22nd.

I hope Josh would have liked his profile. Recovery for him meant not being afraid to be open and honest. He would have wanted you, the reader, to know his story—the gritty details as well as the history of his turnaround that made him the person so many loved. He would also have wanted to give away what God gave him. Addicts know, as I've written elsewhere in this book, that only in giving away recovery do you get to keep it.

The only way I can eulogize Josh and try to capture all that his life was about is to quote what the Apostle Paul wrote in 2 Timothy 4:2: "I have fought the good fight."

Josh won *the good fight.*

"EVERLASTING" ISN'T ALWAYS EVERLASTING. MOST EVERYTHING HAS AN END.

Goldenhar syndrome is a defect that produces incomplete development of the ear, nose, soft palate, lip, and jawbone on one side of the face. Its beginning was in the womb for Josh Bryan and it was thought to be everlasting . . . for a time.

It had the opportunity to mar Josh's soul and spirit daily—to be everlasting—but it didn't. It was a battle Josh won.

The tendency is to wax rhapsodic about Josh and make him an inspirational hero . . . to unintentionally engage in sympathy. That would miss the whole point. He became not a handicapped Josh but just Josh. He neither wanted nor needed sympathy. He didn't just "fight the good fight," he *won* the good fight.

He hurdled every obstacle thrown up by Goldenhar like self-consciousness and low self-esteem. Hell, he was in sales with Taylor Made Farm and, at the time of his passing, was Frank Taylor's assistant. It took no time at all to forget Goldenhar with Josh and appreciate his natural congeniality and personality that included a hysterical, dry sense of humor.

If you want to pick a date when "everlasting" came to an end—when he hurdled his biggest obstacles—it began almost four years ago when he took his last drink and ingested his last drug.

Horses played a part in his recovery, and they were always there. He was related to Frank Taylor (Frank's mother and Josh's grandmother are sisters) and Taylor Made Farm was a familiar gathering place for family events. Also, the farm was an automatic source for a summer job for Taylor kids during high school and college. Josh was one of many young family members who spent at least one summer on the end of a shank. But it went way beyond that with Josh.

Reasons for his addiction and why he wound up in SR escape the classic explanations—abuse, neglect, family history, and more. No doubt, fifteen surgeries (the first of which was when he was seven weeks old) had to have affected him. His parents sheltered him as a young person, he admits, and it couldn't be helped, which was understandable. Even at that, he had a fairly normal childhood and adolescence, or as normal as you can have with Goldenhar. If you can accept that drug use and alcohol abuse *is* normal for teenagers, Josh was no different from most kids his age, maybe a little behind his peers.

"I smoked a little pot in high school when I was sixteen or seventeen. I don't think I took my first drink until I was about nineteen or twenty," he told me.

Something may have clicked, though, with that first drink. "I can't really say what possessed me to start drinking. It probably has a lot to do with the people I was hanging around with, wanting to fit in.

"As I look back now, when I took that first drink, I felt really good about myself. I solved some problems that I had internally with confidence or self-esteem or how people think about me. I kind of got that feeling like they say in the Big Book of A.A. (*Alcoholics Anonymous: The Big Book*) . . . 'You have arrived.'"

Some in A.A. believe there are those physiologically or chemically predisposed to alcohol who react to it like an allergy. It almost instantly demands more of the substance after the very first taste. "Looking back on it now, after taking that first drink, I was, you know, kind of doomed to the disease," Josh said.

Attending Western Kentucky University (WKU) close to the Tennessee border in Bowling Green, away from Josh's native Frankfort, Kentucky, gave him his first taste of independence. He said he did what any college student did: "Went to class, studied, worked hard, played hard."

His world, however, would soon cave in there in Bowling Green. Going into his second semester of his first year, his dad was diagnosed with leukemia. He died after only a few months.

Josh turned to alcohol in his grief. "That was a big excuse for me to kind of drink away all my problems."

Soon after, his mother suffered a fall that would cause a fatal aneurysm.

It was a pivotal time for Josh and he thought his life was over at that point. "I kind of shut everybody out," he said.

The next five years after the death of his parents were a virtual blur. He drank by himself, used cocaine almost daily, and drank before he went to work. In two and a half of the five years he was a student at WKU, he was on academic probation more times than he can remember before finally flunking out.

There really was no place for Josh to go then but to central Kentucky and the best of all places: Taylor Made Farm. There, Frank Taylor and his wife, Kim, stepped in to do what they could for Josh. In retrospect, they did *everything*. Josh said they took him under their wings and fostered him.

He loved Frank, who became a mentor to him and also a father. This is what Josh said about him:

"Frank probably has the biggest heart of really anybody I know, and he's the kind of person who will help anybody any way he can.

"Frank, even when he was drinking, I think he knew his purpose in life, and it was to help people and help run the farm. He realized that his main purpose was to serve God."

Josh would add "guardian angel" to Frank's mentor role and especially to Kim. Their home was a haven for him that gave him time and space to swim toward the surface where truth and reality are. Of his time under Frank's roof, he said he heard a little voice telling him, *It's time to grow up*.

His upbringing by parents he loved was also part of his self-dialogue. Their love taught him that he was a better person than how he was living.

The path to sobriety and recovery, however, still lay ahead.

"I think God let me fall enough—not where I would die or kill somebody else—but he let me fall enough to where, in my mind, I could say,

Okay, enough is enough. It's either kill myself with drugs and alcohol or end up in prison or do something better with my life."

He did something better, and it began with a collapse into God's arms.

Here are his words of that moment:

"I was going to work [at Taylor Made] one morning and my car just completely broke down on East Hickman out here. This sense of desperation just went over me. I could just feel it. I got goose bumps and started bawling my eyes out and just kind of praying to the heavens, 'Help me.'"

A week later, God answered that prayer when Frank "kind of nudged" him, as Josh expressed it, toward recovery with a simple question. The two had gotten into the habit of taking walks together. Frank asked him on this particular walk, "Hey, are you ready to get help?"

It shocked Josh as the two had drunk together on more than a few occasions.

That question earned Frank some jewels in his crown in heaven.

"For that to come out of his mouth, I think that really drove it home that I had to do something," Josh said.

"I just saw that as a sign, and I just went for it."

Josh's life took a new direction on a date he will never forget: July 21st, 2020.

He went from the farm to Lexington's Shepherd's House at Frank's suggestion, where he lived for a year and, after achieving sobriety and recovery, served as a house manager under Christian Countzler.

SR was getting its feet on the ground when Josh was leaving a sober living house after his time at the Shepherd's House. His departure coincided with the purchase of the Preston House. He and Christian were the first residents there before men moved in who had graduated from the house on Hummingbird Lane in downtown Lexington. Preston House soon was full and has been ever since.

Josh's family background with stints mucking stalls and other chores around the farm during summer breaks from school easily prepared him for the work of caring for Thoroughbred horses while at Preston.

Back when he was seventeen or eighteen and working on the farm, he got thrown into the yearling division, which the Taylors like to call "trial by fire."

"A lot of people say with the yearlings or with the babies, you gotta have a soft hand. I think a lot of it is God-given talent," Josh said.

He recognized that gift in himself, accompanied by a passion he knew was needed in the horse business. Here is what he had to say about this:

"I related to the horse. I'd watch how they acted and what they were doing and how their mind worked, and I just tried to get really in tune with them. I was willing to do the grunt work and work seven days a week. I was willing to put in the overtime."

It earned him responsibility for his own barn at Taylor Made and, for a time, working as a surgery technician for the famed Rood & Riddle Equine Hospital in Lexington. The horses, however, were where he found his calling, possibly with the most challenging Thoroughbreds on Taylor Made.

"There's a few really, really tough stallions, but for the most part, they'll listen.

"Of course, there is that one in a hundred who want to kill you," he said with characteristic humor.

Recovery helped him see horses as something more than animals.

"I think God put horses in my life even when I was in addiction. I think they helped me get through those really bad times, when I felt like maybe my life was coming to an end.

"I remember when I was still out in addiction, I'd come in the barn at six in the morning just mad at the world, and those horses humbled me pretty quick. If you go in there with a piss-poor attitude and you're mad and angry, they're going to act up. That's firsthand experience for me.

"I really believe a horse senses trauma and what emotion you're going through.

"Everybody has trauma—I understand that—but when these guys from Stable Recovery come in, they're broken down and just kind of emotionally blank or turned off. The horses can sense it."

Josh saw in the horses what few others get to: "a nurturing way. Most have an innate kindness. When you care for them, they will care for you."

It is ironic in the history of SR that Josh was the first director of the School of Horsemanship. He was a big part of SR's story. The school was the foundation and launching pad for SR.

His experience and, more important, his sobriety carved him out a place later in the Taylor Made organization in sales.

He said it was what he wanted to do for the rest of his life and had wanted to even when drinking and drugging. "I always felt peace around the horses."

A part of his real passion was studying Thoroughbred pedigrees and Thoroughbred sales.

He summed up the path of recovery that doesn't always follow sobriety in these words:

"A lot of alcoholics don't understand that even when you quit drinking, life is still going to be life." He said this with a laugh and also wisdom about the distinction between sobriety and recovery. Life is not going to surrender to you just because you put a bottle down.

"I think for me the biggest thing in early recovery that I learned through therapy and counseling and my sponsor was that I had to learn how to be okay with Josh."

What recovery created was Josh. Just simply Josh. A Josh that was more than okay with God but deeply loved and now part of God's family in heaven.

That Josh is everlasting.

Epilogue

Anything is possible. It all comes back to the horse.
Every bit of it comes back to the horse.
— CHRISTIAN COUNTZLER

A major part of the miracle that is Stable Recovery (SR)—rehabilitating men and transforming the homeless into horsemen—is future growth. It is not overstating it to say in the future we may see national and even global replication of addicts and alcoholics doing meaningful work with horses and finding sobriety, recovery, and most important, finding new lives.

Already, SR has launched a satellite, in March of 2024, at WinStar Farm in Versailles (pronounced "Ver-sales" in Kentucky parlance), west of Lexington. It is, like Taylor Made Farm, one of the giants of the Thoroughbred industry in the Bluegrass. WinStar covers 2,500 acres and is home to over seven hundred Thoroughbreds.

It is now home, also, to six men, all SR residents.

The proposition to WinStar was a simple one: We can send you men well-trained in horsemanship from our school ready to hit the ground running with no learning curve. For a farm short on labor, like probably most horse farms in Kentucky, you would think there would be a welcome with open arms. Yes and no. Management was all for it, but others? Not so much with the existing WinStar associates.

"It was more of your barn foreman and groom-level people. They were thinking that we were going to take jobs from family members," said Christian Countzler. The concern stemmed from many WinStar workers living in neighborhoods on the farm with their families. In the minds of many at WinStar, at risk were not just jobs but their homes.

It didn't take long, though, for those fears to dissipate. In fact, according to Christian, the SR house is kind of the anchor neighborhood for WinStar. The SR men haven't displaced existing employees. If anything, they have been a boon to existing workers by lightening the workload. The SR guys, small though they may be in numbers, have become the go-to for anything extra needed with maintenance or construction beyond horse care.

"WinStar was a great way to start and learn what a satellite program would look like and feel like," said Christian. "The key results were whether the men could stay sober, first and foremost, and second, be successful on the farm. It's working."

Critical to WinStar, as well as any future satellite homes, is the regimen and necessary foundation for sobriety and recovery to flourish.

"We knew what was important: community and the brotherhood that develops—having them living together, working together, and recovering together," said Christian. "We knew that it would work any distance away from Taylor Made and from Preston House, which is the hub for everything that goes on.

"There was a concern that they [at WinStar] don't participate in weekday Morning Meditation meetings out there or at Preston," said Christian. They connect, however, with everything else, especially in the evening. "The WinStar guys come and participate with us at Preston. They're still doing the groups; they're still coming to town hall every Thursday."

Exposure to the "mother church" at Preston House sets an example of sobriety followed by sustained recovery. "What it's allowed us to do is kind of show them an example, like, 'Hey guys, this is where you can get if you work really hard.'"

Morning Meditation at 6:00 is the bedrock of the SR program, setting the tone for both the workday and sobriety consciousness while at work. It is coming to WinStar, according to Christian.

"At WinStar right now, we've got two guys on the training track, two guys with broodmares, and one guy working third shift, which is the night shift. They have put them in every spot out there. That means they're not all together, but as soon as we have enough guys to be able to do that, to have a quorum, we will absolutely do Morning Meditation."

Already, Resolute Racing, operating at a farm in Midway, Kentucky, will be opening a home for an undetermined number of SR men. And plans are in the works for satellites at other central Kentucky horse farms.

This will include Spy Coast Farm in Lexington, which is home to breeding and training performance horses, or horses performing in dressage competition and hunter/jumpers, for example.

More significant, Spy Coast will be home to SR's first female residents sometime in 2026. The program will replicate the men's program to help women struggling with substance addiction and alcoholism.

Internally, with existing operations at Taylor Made, one objective is to codify and make more efficient training in the School of Horsemanship. Increased numbers have meant adding a second instructor to the school.

"Our next big goal is to expand the school, to find the right place and the right people to be able to train more men. We need to do that now," Christian said.

There is what he called a bottleneck with assembling residents in more manageable classes. There is a need to reduce the student-to-teacher ratio for maximum time efficiency and content transfer. "We don't want more than four in a barn at a time. Four is pushing it, really."

Almost as amazing as the results of SR is the support of the horse industry in and around Lexington. The first year of a fundraising gala, SR received a little over $60,000 in funds, not a small sum for a program only months old at the time. It pales in comparison to the 2024 gala, which netted an astonishing $439,000 in contributions.

Critical to the generosity of friends, neighbors, and, yes, competitors of Taylor Made is the understanding that SR can be a resource for sober, reliable workers.

"They see the value and the resource potential. They know it can help them with their workforce," said Christian.

The future for SR involves a natural progression and also a major expansion beyond horse farms into a larger realm. Will Walden's Ready Made Stable began in early 2022 with only SR residents working with the horses. The success of these men gave Christian and Frank Taylor the idea of branching out into the dormitory domiciles on racetrack grounds.

Alcoholism is rampant at every racetrack, with little to combat it beyond chaplaincy programs at each track. SR would be a resource for racetracks needing reliable help in maintenance and other tasks, particularly when a track is dark, or not racing.

A major development later in 2025 is the opening of a new home on the grounds of Keeneland Race Course for year-round maintenance workers. Residents will first complete the School of Horsemanship and then enter maintenance training developed specifically for Keeneland. Once completed, residents will become full-time employees of the racetrack.

In horse racing, past performance is the key indicator of future racetrack success. A great horse wins a maiden special weight race as a two-year-old, then they win allowance races, followed by stakes races graded into listed, and, more significant, Grade 1, 2, and 3 races with escalating purses. The pinnacle in Grade 1 is the Triple Crown races: Kentucky Derby, Preakness, and Belmont Stakes, along with other races like the Travers Stakes at Saratoga in the summer and Breeders' Cup races in November each year.

Ironically, past performance is the key indicator for what can be the future for SR. Christian Countzler shakes his head at the incredible success and fast growth of SR. It is impossible to predict and, more important, limit what the future holds.

"Anything is possible. It all comes back to the horse. Every bit of it comes back to the horse."

Afterword

When [you're] in that coherent state [a] signal goes from the heart to the brain, and it changes what's going on in the brain. [Your] memory improves, your cognition improves, your emotional regulation improves, your health improves.

—DR. ANN BALDWIN

D
r. Baldwin is a retired professor of physiology at the University of Arizona and an expert in studying and evaluating methods to reduce mental and emotional stress. One focus for her has been the study of heart rate variability of horses and humans. HRV, defined most simply, measures the time between heart beats. Variations reflect changes in physical and mental health—reaction to stress, for example. Her experience has included leading one of the few research teams in the world studying synchronous changes in HRV of horse-human pairs and the transfer of physiological information between horse and human.

As you have read in the stories of the men of Stable Recovery (SR), horses have an amazing ability to change human hearts and minds mentally and socially, altering ingrained behaviors, attitudes, emotions, *lives*. Thanks to Dr. Baldwin, we know that those changes are measurable physiologically and that they support the psychological and emotional impact on humans by horses.

This is how she explained synchronization:

"If you're in a very balanced, calm frame of mind or mood, your heart rate will go up when you breathe in and down as you breathe out. So it will oscillate. Horses can pick up on that.

"We've discovered that horses have a very, very slow rhythm, much slower than the normal human rhythm of heart rate variability. So maybe their heart rate will go down and up and down again, maybe three times in one minute, whereas for humans, it's more likely for the heart to oscillate six or seven times in one minute.

"What we found is that when people bond with horses, the human heart rate variability synchronizes with the horse. The rhythm of change of the heart rate, or oscillation, gets slower and synchronizes exactly with the horses." In short, a human heart will slow to match the three oscillations of a horse.

The phenomenon of synchronization between a half-ton horse and a human who weighs, say, 170 pounds is astounding. Consider other differences between horse and human: A horse's heart weighs eight to nine pounds and beats twenty-eight to forty-six times per minute while at rest. A man's heart weighs ten to eleven ounces, while a woman's is eight to nine ounces. The normal resting heart rate for an adult ranges from sixty to one hundred beats per minute. Yet, the difference in heart rate for horse and human is not a factor in horse-human synchronization.

Synchronization indicates what Dr. Baldwin and others studying this phenomenon term a "coherent state" in humans—a state of quietness and calm absent of fear with the horse. It enables another signal from the heart in the human, according to Dr. Baldwin.

"When [you're] in that coherent state [a] signal goes from the heart to the brain, and it changes what's going on in the brain. [Your] memory improves, your cognition improves, your emotional regulation improves, your health improves."

The heart produces an electromagnetic field and a pulsing of this field, said Dr. Baldwin. "We think this is what the horses are picking up."

There are monitors that indicate when a coherent state exists with a human in the presence of a horse. What can happen after that state begins is astonishing.

"I've got videos of someone in that coherent state," said Dr. Baldwin, adding that it automatically gets a horse's attention. "Often [a horse will] just come over to you because they know that you are in a state where you're not going to do them any harm and you're pleasant to be with."

Her research points to the stronger electromagnetic field of a horse compared to a human as one reason for synchronization. "We find that the amplitude of it [with a horse]—how much the heart rate goes up and how much it goes down in one breath—is huge, much bigger than for a human." This could explain why it is the human's HRV that synchronizes to the horse rather than the other way around or both rates meeting somewhere in the middle.

HRV in a herd is also a physiological communicator between horses. If a prey animal approaches a herd, the first horse that senses it will experience a change in HRV—an increase from three variations in a minute to many more. This cues an increase in the variability of all the other horses in a herd and a flight response.

"A herd is one unit. You will have in a herd what's called 'sentinel' horses," Dr. Baldwin said. "They even take turns as sentinels within a herd."

Strangely, it is not uncommon to hear around a barn advice for a worker to "get your heart rate down" to either overcome fear of a horse or to deal with a difficult horse.

Science, as it always seems to do, provides an explanation for what happens in a phenomenon. Where it leaves off is the *why*. Why does a horse respond automatically with kindness or calmness to a human in the coherent state? How can they sense that this makes that human safe? More important from the human perspective, why does this change in HRV produce improvement in memory, cognition, emotional regulation, and health?

For the time being, and perhaps for all time, all we can know is that it is real and it changes those temporarily in the company of a horse.

As well, for the men profiled in this book, the horses provide something expressed in two words coined by Christian Countzler . . . Stable Recovery.

Where Are They Now?

JOSH FRANKS	Broodmare division manager, Taylor Made Farm
TYLER MAXWELL	Exercise rider, WinStar Farm
ROBERT OSBOURN	Director of fundraising and outreach, Stable Recovery
MIKE LOWERY	Farm manager, Diamond A Farm (a division of Taylor Made)
JOHN BOWMAN	Program manager, Stable Recovery
KYLE BERRYMAN	Stable Recovery resident after two stints as assistant trainer for Ready Made Stable
ROGER SULLIVAN	House manager, Stable Recovery
WILL JACKSON	Facilities manager, Stable Recovery
BLANE SERVIS	Assistant trainer, Brad Cox Racing
ROBERT YOUNG	House manager, Stable Recovery
JOHN DAUGHERTY	Yearling groom, Resolute Farm

About the Author

A famous individual, a success in a certain field, who will go unnamed and is now deceased, once said everybody learns to write in the second grade and then they move on. That was true, I'm sure, in his case. For me, eleventh grade English and Miss Douthit *moved* me. High school in Virginia meant lots of Edgar Allan Poe, like Young Pioneers in Russia were force-fed Karl Marx back in the day. Inspiration could only pass you by if you were asleep. That guy was *good*. Class assignments became adventures in ink for me that set a hook from which I'd never wriggle free.

Newspaper writing, I thought, was the future until advertising copywriting came along with a class in journalism school at the University of Missouri on television commercials. A copywriter's pay versus that of reporters sealed the deal. It was off to an ad agency and a veritable writing sandbox.

Magazine writing somehow got into the mix and what God and journalism school intended for me. How do I know God got involved? Spend a little time around the backside of a racetrack and you'll understand.

I say this often and I mean it: I love the smell of urine-soaked straw and horse poo. Today and probably for the duration I will be writing about the source of that smell and the people who race, groom, and train horses. They've never worked a day in their life and neither have I. Being around Thoroughbreds and the people who race them is more than enough and it is not work.

I never envisioned a book that would take me deep into what horses can do for people, specifically the men of Stable Recovery. The horses mirror the men's moods; lead them to self-discovery; affirm them probably for the first time in their lives; put them in a focused present neither regretting the past nor dreading the future; give them purpose replacing aimlessness; and save their lives.

In spite of the gravitas of this book, I am, as I wrote in the Acknowledgments, a word schlep. I don't take myself too seriously. The best accolades I can get are "You got it right" and "The check's in the mail."

At the time of writing, I am about to enter Eastern Kentucky University's graduate school for a master in fine arts degree in creative writing in their very fine Bluegrass Writers Studio. To quote the late, great baseball pitcher Satchel Paige, "Don't look back, something might be gaining on you." There's only one thing to do instead.

Move.